Library of Presidential Rhetoric

Martin J. Medhurst, General Editor

FDR AND FEAR ITSELF

FDR
and Fear Itself

The First Inaugural Address

DAVIS W. HOUCK

Texas A&M University Press : College Station

The paper used in this book meets the minimum requirements
of the American National Standard for Permanence
of Paper for Printed Library Materials, z39.48-1984.
Binding materials have been chosen for durability.

Material from the Raymond Moley Papers is used with permission
of the Hoover Institution Archives.

Frontispiece : FDR delivering the first Inaugural Address.
Courtesy the Franklin D. Roosevelt Presidential Library.

Library of Congress Cataloging-in-Publicaion Data

Houck, Davis W.
    FDR and fear itself : the first inaugural addresss / Davis W. Houck.
        p. cm. — Library of Presidential Rhetoric
    Includes bibliographical references and index.
    ISBN 1–58544–197–x (cloth : alk. paper) —
    ISBN 1–58544–198–8 (pbk. : alk. paper)
    1. United States—Politics and government—1933–1945.
2. Roosevelt, Franklin D. (Franklin Delano), 1882–1945—Oratory.
3. Speeches, addresses, etc., American   4. Roosevelt, Franklin D.
(Franklin Delano), 1882–1945—Friends and associates.
I. Title. II. Series.
E742.5.R65   2002
352.23'86'097309043—dc21   2001008550

Contents

Preface

In my attempts to get as close as possible to the protagonists in the remarkable story of Franklin D. Roosevelt's first inaugural address, I have resorted exclusively to primary historical materials. Those materials can be found in private and public archives, published anthologies, documentary histories, oral histories, autobiographies, and as quotations in secondary sources. On occasion, I have used then contemporary newspapers or periodicals.

In order to avoid undue interference in the reading of the text, I have used repetitive endnotes as sparingly as possible. Noncited quotations refer to an earlier citation in the same chapter.

To my knowledge, eight drafts of the first inaugural address have survived: three outline drafts and five text versions. Only the final reading copy that Roosevelt delivered on March 4, 1933 is reprinted here. As the reader will note, several additional drafts were either deliberately destroyed or did not survive.

Many institutions and people had a direct hand in shaping this project. The Council on Research and Creativity at Florida State University provided generous summer grant money that enabled me to visit several archives. Stephen Langloise was instrumental in securing my visiting fellow status at the Hoover Institution. I am especially grateful to the staffs of the Roosevelt Presidential Library, the Hoover Presidential Library, and the Hoover Institution for helping me locate important primary source materials.

Several friends and colleagues offered helpful commentary on earlier drafts. To Bob Luce, Kay Picart, Marty Medhurst, Chet Weigle, and Barry Sapolsky, my thanks for your encouragement and editorial care.

And to my father, Bill Houck, and to my sister, Sharon Houck, thanks for spending part of your Christmas vacations reading a book that you otherwise would not have. Thanks also, "Sue," for gamely braving the archival minefield by photocopying the Moley diary. Carol "Pokey-mama" Weigle was of great help in tracking down Aiken, South Carolina, local history related to FDR's paramour, Lucy Mercer Rutherfurd, who wintered there with her family.

A special thanks is in order to my research assistant at Florida State, Mihaela Nocasian. For scouring miles of microfilm in order to give this project its intimate detail and for the care in which you recorded it all, I will be forever in your debt. So, too, will the readers of this book.

I also have Marty Medhurst to thank for his vision in helping to create the Library of Presidential Rhetoric at Texas A&M University Press, of which this project is the inaugural volume. Your personal invitation to participate will not soon be forgotten—nor will the myriad outlets for young scholars' work that you have personally opened over the years.

Finally, just a brief note to my teachers—Chet Weigle, Amos Kiewe, Carole Blair, and Dick Gregg—to whom this book is dedicated. I could never have told this remarkable story without your tutelage, care, and patience over the years. Our story is also here in these pages.

FDR AND FEAR ITSELF

Franklin D. Roosevelt's
First Inaugural Address

President Hoover, Mr. Chief Justice, my friends. This is a day of national consecration, and I am certain that on this day my fellow Americans expect that on my induction into the Presidency I will address them with a candor and a decision which the present situation of our people impels. This is preeminently the time to speak the truth, the whole truth, frankly and boldly. Nor need we shrink from honestly facing conditions in our country today. This great nation will endure as it has endured, will revive, and will prosper. So, first of all, let me assert my firm belief that the only thing we have to fear is fear itself—nameless, unreasoning, unjustified terror which paralyzes needed efforts to convert retreat into advance.

In every dark hour of our national life, a leadership of frankness and of vigor has met with that understanding and support of the people themselves which is essential to victory. And I am convinced that you will again give that support to leadership in these critical days.

In such a spirit on my part and on yours we face our common difficulties. They concern, thank God, only material things. Values have shrunk to fantastic levels, taxes have risen, our ability to pay has fallen, government of all kinds is faced by serious curtailment of income, the means of exchange are frozen in the currents of trade, the withered leaves of industrial enterprise lie on every side, farmers find no markets for their produce, and the savings of many years in thousands of families are gone. More important, a host of unemployed citizens face the grim problem of existence, and an equally great number toil with little return. Only a foolish optimist can deny the dark realities of the moment.

And yet our distress comes from no failure of substance. We are stricken by no plague of locusts. Compared with the perils which our forefathers conquered, because they believed and were not afraid, we have still much to be thankful for. Nature still offers her bounty, and human efforts have multiplied it. Plenty is at our doorstep, but a generous use of it languishes in the very sight of the supply. Primarily, this is because the rulers of the exchange of mankind's goods have failed through their own stubbornness and their own incompetence, have admitted their failure, and have abdicated. Practices of the unscrupulous money-changers stand indicted in the court of public opinion, rejected by the hearts and minds of men.

True, they have tried, but their efforts have been cast in the pattern of an outworn tradition. Faced by failure of credit, they have proposed only the lending of more money. Stripped of the lure of profit by which to induce our people to follow their false leadership, they have resorted to exhortations, pleading tearfully for restored confidence. They only know the rules of a generation of self-seekers. They have no vision, and when there is no vision the people perish.

Yes, the money-changers have fled from their high seats in the temple of our civilization. We may now restore that temple to the ancient truths. The measure of that restoration lies in the extent to which we apply social values more noble than mere monetary profit. Happiness lies not in the mere possession of money; it lies in the joy of achievement, in the thrill of creative effort. The joy, the moral stimulation, of work no longer must be forgotten in the mad chase of evanescent profits. These dark days, my friends, will be worth all they cost us if they teach us that our true destiny is not to be ministered unto but to minister to ourselves, to our fellowmen.

Recognition of that falsity of material wealth as the standard of success goes hand in hand with the abandonment of the false belief that public office and high political position are to be valued only by the standards of pride of place and personal profit. And there must be an end to a conduct in banking and in business which too often has given to a sacred trust the likeness of callous and selfish wrongdoing. Small wonder that confidence languishes, for it thrives only on honesty, on honor, on the sacredness of obligations, on faithful protection, and on unselfish performance. Without them, it cannot live.

Restoration calls, however, not for changes in ethics alone. This nation is asking for action, and action now.

Our greatest primary task is to put people to work. This is no unsolvable problem if we face it wisely and courageously. It can be accomplished in part by direct recruiting by the government itself, treating the task as we would treat the emergency of a war but at the same time, through this employment, accomplishing great—greatly needed projects to stimulate and reorganize the use of our great natural resources.

Hand in hand with that we must frankly recognize the overbalance of population in our industrial centers and by engaging on a national scale in a redistribution endeavor to provide a better use of the land for those best fitted for the land. Yes, the task can be helped by definite efforts to raise the values of agricultural products and with this the power to purchase the output of our cities. It can be helped by preventing realistically the tragedy of the growing loss through forecl—foreclosure of our small homes and our farms. It can be helped by insistence that the Federal, the State, and the local governments act forthwith on the demand that their cost be drastically reduced. It can be helped by the unifying of relief activities which today are often scattered, uneconomical, unequal. It can be helped by national planning for and supervision of all forms of transportation and of communications and other utilities that have a definitely public character. There are many ways in which it can be helped, but it can never be helped by merely talking about it.

We must act, we must act quickly.

[5]

And finally, in our progress towards a resumption of work we require two safeguards against a return of the evils of the old order. There must be a strict supervision of all banking and credits and investments. There must be an end to speculation with other people's money. And there must be provision for an adequate but sound currency.

These, my friends, are the lines of attack. I shall presently urge upon a new Congress, in special session, detailed measures for their fulfillment, and I shall seek the immediate assistance of the forty-eight states.

Through this program of action we address ourselves to putting our own national house in order and making income balance outgo. Our international trade relations, though vastly important, are in point of time and necessity secondary to the establishment of a sound national economy. I favor as a practical policy the putting of first things first. I shall spare no effort to restore world trade by international economic readjustment, but the emergency at home cannot wait on that accomplishment. The basic thought that guides these specific means of national recovery is not nationally—narrowly nationalistic. It is the insistence, as a first consideration, upon the interdependence of the various elements in and parts of the United States of America, a recognition of the old and permanently important manifestation of the American spirit of the pioneer. It is the way to recovery. It is the immediate way. It is the strongest assurance that recovery will endure.

In the field of world policy I would dedicate this nation to the policy of the "good neighbor"—the neighbor who resolutely respects himself and, because he does so, respects the rights of others—the neighbor who respects his obligations and respects the sanctity of his agreements in and with a world of neighbors.

If I read the temper of our people correctly, we now realize as we have never realized before our interdependence on each other, that we cannot merely take but we must give as well, that if we are to go forward, we must move as a trained and loyal army, willing to sacrifice for the good of a common discipline, because without such discipline no progress can be made, no leadership becomes effective. We are, I know, ready and willing to submit our lives and our property to such discipline because it makes possible a leadership which aims at the larger good. This I propose to offer, pledging that the larger purposes will bind upon us, bind upon us all as a sacred obligation, with a unity of duty hitherto evoked only in times of armed strife.

With this pledge taken, I assume unhesitatingly the leadership of this great army of our people dedicated to a disciplined attack upon our common problems.

Action in this image, action to this end, is feasible under the form of government which we have inherited from our ancestors. Our constitution is so simple, so practical, that it is possible always to meet extraordinary needs by changes in emphasis and arrangement without loss of essential form. That is why our constitutional system has proved itself the most superbly enduring political mechanism the modern world has ever seen. It has met every stress of vast expansion of territory, of foreign wars, of bitter internal strife, of world relations. And it is to be hoped that the normal balance of executive and legislative authority may be wholly equal, wholly adequate, to meet the unprecedented task before us. But it may be that an unprecedented demand and need for undelayed action may call for temporary departure from that normal balance of public procedure. I am prepared under my constitutional duty to recommend the measures that a stricken nation in the midst of a stricken world may require. These measures, or such other measures as the Congress may build out of its experience and wisdom, I shall seek within my constitutional authority to bring to speedy adoption. But in the event that the Congress shall fail to take one of these two courses, in the event that the national emergency is still critical, I shall not evade the clear course of duty that will then confront me. I shall ask the Congress for the one remaining instrument to meet the crisis: broad executive power to wage a war against the emergency, as great as the power that would be given to me if we were in fact invaded by a foreign foe.

For the trust reposed in me I will return the courage and the devotion that befit the time. I can do no less.

We face the arduous days that lie before us in the warm courage of national unity, with the clear consciousness of seeking old and precious moral values, with the clean satisfaction that comes from the stern performance of duty by old and young alike. We aim at the assurance of a rounded, a permanent national life. We do not distrust the essen—the future of essential democracy. The people of the United States have not failed. In their need they have registered a mandate that they want direct, vigorous action. They have asked for discipline and direction under leadership. They have made me the present instrument of their wishes. In the spirit of the gift, I take it.

In this dedication of a nation, we humbly ask the blessing of God. May he protect each and every one of us. May he guide me in the days to come.

CHAPTER ONE

March 4, 1933

"In this dedication of a nation, we humbly ask the blessing of God. May he protect each and every one of us. May he guide me in the days to come."

With this final appeal to the Almighty, at precisely 1:34 P.M., the estimated audience of one hundred thousand gathered before the Capitol on the cold, gray Saturday burst into thunderous applause. To Raymond Moley and those seated not far behind the nation's thirty-second president, the applause seemed to come in great waves, slowly surging before reaching its crest at the Capitol's steps. It was powerful, even perhaps a bit threatening. He, too, broke into hearty applause along with the assembled crowd.

As he clapped, he might have reflected on whether the story would ever come out—would this clapping multitude and the millions no doubt clapping hard by their radios around the nation ever know the true story of this inaugural address? Would his role in its drafting ever be acknowledged? But was this really the time and place to be entertaining such self-aggrandizing thoughts?

He needed to find his way over to the president's inaugural parade reviewing stand. He eyed the heavy cardboard ticket carefully, and then smiled. It read: "Gate 3, Section C, Row 6, Seat 18." Not bad for a fellow who had worked intimately with the nation's now most powerful man for all of a year.

• • •

As the applause slowly died down to the point where she could take the measure of her own voice, Sarah Love just had to say something— to someone, anyone. She turned to the stranger standing politely next to her, and said enthusiastically, "Any man who can talk like that in times like these is worthy of every ounce of support a true American has."[1] The nameless man replied to the young school teacher from Wilmington, North Carolina, with grave conviction: "I didn't vote for him, but he's my man, and any man who won't back him now isn't worthy of the name of an American." She nodded eagerly.

Something had clearly changed—something fundamental, almost material, real—in the mere span of those 1,929 words. The speech had been heard, as all speeches might be. But it had a weightier quality to it; it was a speech first and foremost to be experienced, felt. Across the country, people had clearly absorbed the resonant cadences of their new president, Franklin D. Roosevelt, into the very marrow of their bones. "Your voice," wrote F. W. Clements of Rochester, "carried more conviction and inspired more confidence in the people than could page after page of the printed word. It's your voice that the people want to listen to."

"Never, since the news of the Armistice reached this country, have I had such a vibrant and electric feeling come over me, as when you made your inaugural address," confessed Albert C. Davies of Rutherford, New Jersey. Morris Sterns of Columbus, Georgia, also experienced this energized feeling. "This noon your inaugural address electrified us! Its clarity, logic and sincerity struck us with the force and simplicity of Lincoln's Speech at Gettysburg." Dorothy Fullinger of Brandenton, Florida, also felt its palpable touch: "After listening to your touching inaugural address, I felt as if I could stretch out my arms and cry: 'I'm glad I'm an American!' It gave me a new thrill in life, something to live for."

Raymond Hummel of Cleveland was also moved to report to the president the material effects of his words: "To-day sitting among a gathering of the all but 'forgotten men' during your inaugural address, I seen those worried looks replaced by smiles and confidence, eyes fill up with tears of gratitude, shoulders lifted and chest out." "Everywhere one goes," wrote Herbert Siegel of New York City, "one cannot but feel the easing of tension, which was so prevalent only a few days ago."

As Joseph Williams of Detroit listened to the speech on the radio, "a feeling almost impossible to describe came over me. It was a feeling of renewed hope, a feeling that this old world is again going to be a pretty good place after all, a feeling that soon this life will be worth living." Ilse Tierney of Seattle was one of the fortunate few who witnessed the speech "through the eyes of NBC and Columbia [CBS]." The effect was much the same: "we feel as though we 'had been lifted up.' The 'new note' emphasized in the broadcast was so apparent, so tangible that we feel, literally, as though we had gone through a much longed for portal into a Promised Land."

Hope, confidence, optimism, and faith—these were the emotions and feelings recorded and sent to Franklin Roosevelt by the citizens of the nation in the immediate aftermath of the address. They were felt and expressed in bodily terms, perhaps in a way that only a recovering paralytic might intuitively understand and appreciate. But there was something more to the nation's collective response, something far more fundamental than mere emotions, and something far more important than even a bodily identification. Those 1,929 words could only have had their origins in the transcendent—no, the Divine. It was a lineal Divinity that extended from the Pentateuch of Moses on to Joshua and then to Jesus Christ. It was also a civic Divinity that extended from Washington to Jefferson, on through to Lincoln. Its mantel was now clearly on the shoulders of the man who promised to expel the money changers from the nation's temple.

"After hearing your utterances," wrote Percy Viosca of New Orleans, "I felt as though at this critical period of our Nation's existence our God, as he had done before, had sent at the exact time, a man who possessed the prudence of a Washington, the intelligence of a Jefferson, the wisdom of a Lincoln." Rector Edmund Trotman of Asbury Park, New Jersey, wrote, "it is with grateful heart to Almighty God for his selection of a modern Joshua to lead his people in the great crisis." George Townsend of Chicago also noted the Old Testament parallels: "The Almighty ruler always sends a Moses at his appointed time and a united people now rejoices at his coming and knows that our 'Forward march' began the very moment your final words were spoken."

Letter upon letter came flooding into the nation's capital, convinced that this man so many had doubted during the campaign season—a man many pundits had derogatorily deemed an intellectual lightweight, an affable country gentleman—had now taken his place among God's chosen few. Elizabeth Ehrlich of New York City expressed what surely many were feeling: "I feel as thousands of others must feel while hearing your magnificent speech, that you are inspired and permeated by the spirit of the Great 'Almighty' himself and that your success during the next four years is assured through that power." Mrs. William Showalter of Westmont, New Jersey, went one step farther as she sought to understand a Roosevelt presidency: "I am quite sure it was not a mere bit of chance that brought you to the office you now hold. I truly believe you have been sent directly by god to our nation, for such a time as this."

And so it was that, by popular agreement, Franklin Roosevelt had been sent by the God of Moses and Joshua, the Father of the Redeemer, the same God, of course, who had blessed His chosen nation in its most dire hour with a Washington and a Lincoln. All this in 1,929 words. Some looked just a bit past the words to find the source of Roosevelt's election. It was not to be found in policy, or even in pedigree. And it certainly was not in promises; the nation had experienced far too many promises. Rather, the eloquence of March 4 was a proof—*the* proof—that the events of three weeks earlier had not occurred by chance.

At Miami's Bay Front Park, perched conspicuously atop the backseat of an open-canopied car, the president-elect had addressed a large but informal gathering of Floridians. The bullets of a would-be assassin were deflected from their very exposed and proximate target at the last split second. Combined with the inaugural address, the events in Miami were explicable only as Divine intervention: God intended that Franklin Roosevelt save the nation. Nelson Ehrlich wrote: "Thanks be to God that you were spared in Miami. My first thought then was that you were destined to achieve your lofty purpose as a factor in these dark days." Ike Spellman of New York City agreed: "'God' was with you in spareing you from that terrible incident at Miami, Florida last month, and I have all the confidence in the world in you." Joseph Williams came to a similar conclusion: "Just as God made You the President of the American people, as He preserved You at Miami, I feel sure that He has destined You to be the Saviour of Our Country." The eloquent inaugural address was simply one more manifestation of God's call.

However, beyond predestination, many wrote forebodingly to the new president and enjoined upon him their understanding of what a Divine mandate to lead meant. They had heard as much from many of their elected officials over the past month. At that crucial moment, when unemployment neared 25 percent, when big and small banks across the nation were closed to their desperate depositors, and with the soup lines extending ever farther, democracy interfered with theology. Congressional deliberation in the midst of Heaven-sent declaration was heretical. The mandate was obvious. "May I suggest," wrote Long Island's Joseph D'Angelo, "that what America needs to-day is a dictator, which I believe you can be, while not hurting the people. We all have faith in your judgment." Daniel Boone Herring of Los Angeles linked the religious with the scientific: "The secret of your appeal to the people of the United States and to the world, lies in the simple, unfeigned prayer you uttered at the close of your inaugural address." He continued, "Science has given you the radio—a medium through which you may speak to the world. Use it. Continue to use it even though you must confiscate it and make it a government agency and deny private use of it."

Advice also came in a telegram from A. Hechscher: "With hesitation and diffidence permit me to suggest the appointment of five dictators or rather subdictators. Designate these for one year at a time modestly paid but with full supervisory control over industry and commerce labor farming finance and transportation." Margaret Jones of West Reading, Pennsylvania, linked the civic and the religious: "I want more power for the Presidency. The power is yours, we are all with you in one accord. To be relieved from the shackles of slavery, we need a strong man, a Moses or a Lincoln or a Washington to head the way." She concluded with Roosevelt's own inaugural language: "May god bless you Mr. Roosevelt and take your lash in hand and drive them [money changers] from their dens. And bring the gold out of its hiding places."

In just twenty minutes, Franklin Roosevelt had managed with 1,929 words to persuade many of his near-Divine status and calling. Clearly, this was not just about his words—as eloquent as they were. Clearly, these were desperate people writing, people only too willing to see the Divine hand of material salvation at work. For too long they had not seen it. And so perhaps they collectively wondered: had God abandoned His chosen land and chosen people? Why was He willing—no, stipulating—that they suffer so? Did not the very efficacy of capitalism somehow go hand in hand with those godly virtues of sacrifice and work and thrift? Maybe it was not about them at all. Maybe this God, who seemed to favor democracy and freedom and justice foremost among the world's nations, was exacting retribution for Wall Street's money changers. Had not their new president said as much? He promised to vanquish them from the temple. But were those mere metaphors? For A. H. Woods of Connellsville, Pennsylvania, and no doubt for many of the silent voices that he represented, the country had no time for troping misery. "By your own words I am led to believe that you are not so much affected by the wisdom of men as by the power of God. Therefore I sincerely hope that congress will allow you many dictatorial powers."

On March 4, Raymond Moley could not have known that the words he and Roosevelt had painstakingly crafted would register in such theological and antidemocratic terms. He did know, though, that the text he had worked diligently on, dating back nearly six months to a hotel room in San Francisco, would not be remembered as his. No, Franklin Roosevelt would see to it that his signature and persona were firmly affixed to this profoundly important state paper. The political scientist from Olmsted Falls, Ohio, had no illusions when it came to such matters as power and public memory.

As he turned and headed away from the Capitol, walking briskly toward the reviewing stand, he figured that someday—who knew when?—his role in crafting the new president's first speech would be recognized, and perhaps even applauded.

He had already seen to it.

CHAPTER TWO

September 22, 1932

Ray Moley was not quite sure what to think. Maybe the party's "heavies," who had dutifully trouped to Albany and Hyde Park following Roosevelt's nomination on the fourth ballot at Chicago, had been right after all. Maybe the candidate should have stayed home, sequestered from the vicissitudes and treacheries of the campaign trail. Instead, Roosevelt insisted on making a cross-country train trip, which began on September 12, 1932. He also insisted on frequent stops and speeches at places most people had never heard of, let alone visited—places such as Goodland, Kansas; Cache Junction, Utah; McCamron, Idaho; and Lima, Montana. Just how many votes were there to be won at places such as Lamy, New Mexico? And what about the candidate's health? Many in and out of the party wondered—sometimes aloud—whether all the whispering about the effects of infantile paralysis contained a kernel of truth. And what about Roosevelt's decision to spend so much time in California, traversing the state almost from top to bottom? Had he not learned anything about the perilous politics of the Golden State from Republican candidate Charles Evans Hughes' miscalculations in 1916?

Just ten days into the trip and on their way into California, Moley was already feeling the strain. His was a most onerous job: writing speeches, coordinating drafts of speeches, conferring with Roosevelt on all of these drafts, balancing egos, glad-handing with the incessant stream of politicians seeking face time with the candidate aboard the Roosevelt Special, and trying to stay in touch with the party's headquarters back in New York City.

On top of this long list of political duties was a more mundane concern: September 22 was going to be a real scorcher of a day. As the train pulled into Redding at the north end of the central valley at approximately 11:09 A.M., the temperature was already well over ninety degrees—on its way, said the local papers, into triple digits. How would Roosevelt handle the heat, to say nothing of the four speeches he was slated to deliver? Maybe the candidate would handle it better than he would; after all, Roosevelt had spent considerable time in the steamy South—both at Warm Springs, Georgia, where he had convalesced for nearly eight years, and in the tropics of south Florida, where he had once co-owned a houseboat.

Moley presently returned to his pen and paper; he needed to finish a speech in time for the late afternoon stop at the capital in Sacramento. The one man whom they could not afford to overlook in the state was the venerable but highly unpredictable Hiram Johnson. Roosevelt and Moley knew that Progressives within the Republican Party—George Norris of Nebraska, William Borah of Idaho, Robert La Follette of Wisconsin, and Johnson—were inclined to vote for the Democratic ticket, but neither man was counting their votes at this point. Moley scribbled just a bit obsequiously on his legal pad, "a warrior in the ranks of true American progress." After the stenographer typed up Moley's draft, Roosevelt, as was his penchant, added and deleted terms and phrases in his characteristic penciled script.

Despite the hundred-plus-degree heat in Sacramento, Roosevelt delivered the encomium to Johnson without incident. The speech clearly pleased the former governor, now serving as a senator. Herbert Hoover's adopted home state increasingly looked to be leaning Roosevelt's way. But this was no time for congratulations; Moley had an even more important rhetorical task confronting him.

As the Roosevelt Special departed Sacramento at 4:15 that afternoon, headed toward the Oakland Pier and then San Francisco, Moley turned his attention to a lengthy speech drafted by fellow Columbia University professor Adolph A. Berle Jr. (pronounced Ber-lee). Together with Moley and another Columbia professor, Rexford Tugwell, Berle was a member of the preconvention Roosevelt team—a small group designated by Roosevelt, the inveterate nicknamer, as his privy council. Later in the primary season, the *New York Times'* James Kieran relabeled them the Brains Trust. The name stuck.

Back in mid-August, Berle had sent the governor a three-page, single-spaced memorandum urging him to articulate "a guiding philosophical statement" in the event that he won the general election.[1] Roosevelt wrote back and urged Berle to work on such a statement. The draft Berle had written was sent to Moley as he headed west aboard the Roosevelt Special.

Seated next to Moley as the train chugged westward toward land's end was Nevada senator Key Pittman, who was serving as a sort of liaison with western politicos. Together, Moley and Pittman read Berle's draft. Roosevelt had told Moley earlier in the trip that all he needed to do in San Francisco was greet his listeners kindly and congratulate them on the Golden Gate Bridge.[2] This was one of the few times that the candidate's political and rhetorical instincts were wrong.

Moley had been informed earlier in the day by California newspapermen that Roosevelt should not address the Commonwealth Club with the general campaign banalities; it was much too sophisticated a political group for such fare. Perhaps this audience was the appropriate gathering for Berle's high-minded philosophical statement.

There was only one problem, though. Time. Moley simply did not have enough of it to engage in a careful editing of the lengthy, carefully argued draft. He and Pittman thus made only minor stylistic changes. As the train pulled into San Francisco, Moley had the stenographer type up the speech. Roosevelt had yet to see what was intended to be his "guiding philosophical statement."

This tendency—no, by now more of a habit—of Roosevelt's to allow other people such access and influence worried Moley. How could a man on the threshold of the nation's most powerful elected position allow, and even encourage, those around him to essentially speak for him?

This had worried him all along—at least all of the seven months that he had worked for Roosevelt. He still found it hard to believe that so many of the words that came from the candidate's lips—words that so easily rolled off his tongue as if native, impromptu creations—were from him. What did this seemingly innate ability say about the candidate? What did it say about him? The campaign trail was not the place for existential angst. Not now anyway. Moley's sister, Nell, with whom he was close, could be trusted. He made a mental note to talk about it with her later.

Moley's first campaign-related meeting with Roosevelt had occurred back in January. He had been brought to the governor's attention much earlier, by secretary and long-time political confidante, Louis McHenry Howe. Moley would learn quickly that getting along with the gnomish, asthmatic former newspaperman was absolutely essential to working productively with Roosevelt. In 1928, Howe had enjoined Moley to assist the governor with drafting a campaign speech on New York's criminal justice system, of which the professor was expert. That speech, based largely on Moley's memorandum, had been generally well received.

Roosevelt was exasperated at the January meeting. "Make no mistake about it," he declared, "I don't know why anyone would *want* to be President, with things in the shape they are now."[3] Moley's polite response would have irrevocable consequences: He said he would be delighted to help in any way. Now, just a few months later, he was serving as one of the principal architects of Roosevelt's presidential ambitions.

Roosevelt liked to test those around him, and he immediately put Moley to a major one: writing his first major campaign speech of 1932—a national radio broadcast that would hopefully galvanize support for a Roosevelt candidacy among both Democrats and Republicans. That speech, delivered on April 7, soon came to be known as the "Forgotten Man" address, as Moley had deliberately borrowed the appellation from William Graham Sumner. Generally well received, the speech signified to Roosevelt that Moley had passed his first important test.

Before the speech, Moley was aware of the candidate's need for rhetorical assistance. Roosevelt was not much of a speechwriter. Nor was Howe. The governor's principal speechwriter for state addresses was Samuel I. Rosenman, for whom Howe harbored thinly veiled suspicion and jealousy. Rosenman was fine for New York, but national politics was beyond his pale. Roosevelt had initially experimented with a committee approach to major speeches, but one of those early efforts had fared miserably. Using Howe, Rosenman, and the esteemed Edward M. House, close friend and confidante to Pres. Woodrow Wilson, Roosevelt delivered their joint rhetorical creation to the New York Grange on February 2. Their assignment was admittedly difficult: disavow the candidate's earlier enthusiasm for internationalism while not seeming to capitulate too readily to the isolationist sentiment expressed by some within his own party, most notably by powerful newspaper magnate William Randolph Hearst.

The speech was a disaster. Even wife Eleanor did not speak to him for several days following the carefully concocted kowtowing on display before the Grange—and party leaders.

Then Ray Moley came to the rescue.

On April 12, just five days after the success of the Forgotten Man address, Moley wrote a lengthy letter to his sister. While he was clearly buoyed by his newfound role and by his proximity to fame and fortune, a clear note of circumspection had entered. In response to Nell's query of what the governor "was like," her brother wrote: "I've been amazed with his interest in things. It skips and bounces through seemingly intricate subjects and maybe it is my academic training that makes me feel that no one could possibly learn much in such a hit or miss fashion."[4] The professor continued, "What he gets is from talking to people and when he stores away the net of a conversation he never knows what part he has kept is what he said himself or what his visitor said. There is a lot of autointoxication of the intelligence that we shall have to watch." In brief, Moley worried that Roosevelt was simply too credulous, too accepting, too willing to believe. "The frightening aspect of his methods is F.D.R.'s great receptivity. So far as I know he makes no effort to check up on anything that I or anyone else has told him." Moley then turned reflective: "I wonder what would happen if we should selfishly try to put things over on him. He would find out—but it would be too late." From this he could draw but one conclusion: "This means a hell of a responsibility for me."

By September, Moley had experienced firsthand just what a "hell of a responsibility" it was to keep the candidate from undue influence. Before the Democratic National Convention, the responsibility was comparatively simple to negotiate: the team was small and well coordinated. Louis Howe worked the back channels of arcane party structures via letter and phone, while the amiable Jim Farley was doing interpersonal political work across the country, selling FDR and his candidacy to any willing ear. Moley, Tugwell, and Berle worked at the governor's mansion in Albany or the candidate's stately home in Hyde Park—Springwood—coordinating policy plans and the three major preconvention speeches that Roosevelt delivered. It all seemed to work so easily, almost seamlessly.

But with the nomination, everything changed. All at once, everyone wanted a piece of the candidate. Even as he received his party's nomination in Chicago, the patron of the Democratic Party, Bernard Baruch, and his "spokesman," Gen. Hugh S. Johnson, demanded to see the draft of the speech that the nominee intended to use the following day. Rosenman and Moley were aghast: Roosevelt's win had changed everything. The candidate was no longer "theirs." He was now a party man, a representative. And it was not just "Barney" Baruch who wanted in on the action.

At Topeka, for example, the site of the candidate's first major speech of the train trip, Moley estimated that nearly twenty-five hands had touched the final draft that Roosevelt delivered on farm policy. Little wonder that the press shredded it. From now on, Moley would take no chances; he would try to be in Roosevelt's presence as much as he could. If someone wanted to influence the candidate, Moley would try to ensure that influence would ultimately run through him, a man largely unknown to party regulars.

Moley was amazed at the suffocating crowds lining Market Street in San Francisco. Then again, it seemed to him that the candidate encountered jubilant crowds wherever he went. At junction after junction, in the middle of the night and at the height of the afternoon, enthusiastic crowds came out to get a glimpse of the "recovered" paralytic, the man whose voice seemed to radiate hope and confidence. All these people— all because of what they had read or heard; the care that Moley devoted to each phrase—and these crowds that seemed barely contained at times—somehow the two were related. The words and ideas had indeed reverberated across the country. All those trips to Hyde Park and Albany, all the late-night planning sessions with the candidate and his tiny privy council—all of it was here, now, before his eyes. "Autointoxication" could be a most heady wine.

The candidate had also experienced the crowds, beginning in Cleveland, extending in what seemed like an unbreakable line, all the way to the Pacific Ocean. He had experienced them much more viscerally than Ray Moley ever could.

Now, however, the candidate needed to speak with him.

Roosevelt's suite at the Palace Hotel was crowded with politicians, old friends, and well-wishers on the evening of September 22. Moley tried to stay within earshot of the candidate—all the while meeting and greeting. He was secretly hoping that the crowd would soon disperse. He had work to do with the candidate, and it had been a very long and exhausting day.

Roosevelt had not yet seen the Berle draft, let alone the minor revisions that he and Pittman had made. If nothing else, he figured that Roosevelt needed to familiarize himself with the rhythm of the speech. While Moley knew the candidate to be a master of the manuscript, even masters needed a bit of practice.

As the crowd in the suite finally began to thin, Moley figured that at last he would get some time alone with Roosevelt. He figured wrong. Just as the last visitor left, in breezed Woodrow Wilson's son-in-law, William Gibbs McAdoo. Moley had grown to loathe the former treasury secretary, finding him to be self-important, "officious," in ways that many other party big shots were not.[5]

McAdoo blurted out to Moley that he wanted—needed—to be alone with the candidate. That was just what Moley had hoped to avoid. Fortunately, Roosevelt had witnessed the obnoxious self-important demand. Then again, was not McAdoo entitled to have a moment of privacy with Roosevelt? It was McAdoo, after all, who had announced the release of the California delegates during the pivotal fourth ballot, the one that put Roosevelt over the top at the Democratic National Convention just a few months earlier.

Moley headed down the corridor to his room; it was his first "eviction" in several months. Not long thereafter, though, he heard a knock on his door. He opened it, surprised to find McAdoo in the hallway. In true errand boy fashion, Roosevelt had actually sent him to fetch Moley. The professor suppressed a smile as he could tell by McAdoo's countenance that he had been bested in this game of interpersonal power politics.

When Moley reentered the suite, Roosevelt ordered the telephone cut off. No visitors or well-wishers were to disturb them. After the candidate removed the leather and steel braces from his withered legs, Moley and Roosevelt began their work on the Berle draft. Moley read every sentence aloud. Roosevelt listened attentively, liking what he heard. He would deliver the speech in much the same tone Moley had delivered it to him.

After his reading, Moley figured Roosevelt was ready to call it a day. Instead, the candidate asked him if he would stay just a bit longer. He wanted to talk, not about the campaign—they had done enough of that in recent days. No, he wanted to talk about the future, his future—as president.

Roosevelt was no rookie when it came to reading a crowd. After more than twenty years of it, he was somewhat adept. The faces that he had seen along the three thousand miles of rail they had traveled brought him to the realization that he would be the nation's thirty-second president. He had sensed it in their hopeful expressions and in their earnest calls to him. Moreover, the crowds were bigger than he had anticipated. And Hoover was not even campaigning yet; in fact, he had vowed *not* to campaign.

He began talking to Moley about what he should say on March 4, 1933, at his inauguration. Moley's pulse quickened. He knew that this was Roosevelt's way of seeking rhetorical counsel. He also knew he would be in charge of drafting the inaugural address—of taking the ideas now being articulated at the Palace Hotel suite and transforming them into something eloquent, effective, perhaps even memorable.

At times like these, Moley usually took notes. But not that night. The gravity and the silence enveloping the moment ensured that the conversation would be remembered.

Roosevelt thought ahead. First, the situation in early March would likely resemble something akin to war. Roosevelt and Moley had heard repeatedly the metaphor of war invoked by President Hoover. But war required active, visible leadership—something he had not offered the country. First and foremost, the nation needed to be called to heroic duty. Moley interrupted, suggesting that the word "discipline" seemed appropriate in a crisis as grave as war.[6] He was thinking analogically, not metaphorically. Roosevelt liked the term.

Roosevelt also reflected on the lengthy interregnum between an electoral victory and inauguration—a long four months. He figured that the lame duck Seventy-second Congress—controlled by Democratic and Republican majorities in the House and Senate respectively— would continue the bitter factionalism and gridlock that the nation had witnessed earlier that summer. And Hoover would not be able to lead it. The economy would only worsen in the absence of legislation and in the confusion of uncertainty. By the time Roosevelt arrived in Washington, D. C., the nation would be badly stricken. Moley had already incorporated this metaphor—that of health and sickness—in a number of speeches. He made a mental note to return to it for the inaugural address; it seemed to be a favorite of Roosevelt's.

While the nation would no doubt be very confused by the seeming inability of its brightest minds to fix the problem, they could not be pandered to. Roosevelt expressed in no uncertain terms that they could not sugarcoat the realities of the economic situation. He was particularly adamant on this point: The nation had been lulled by its chief executive, who kept saying that the worst was over, the corner had been turned, that confidence, and thus the economy, was on the rise. Roosevelt would not employ these tactics of optimism in an attempt to create more optimism. There needed to be a leveling with the people—not to weaken their resolve but rather to inject a note of reality and determination into the situation. He aimed for encouragement, not despair. It would be no easy rhetorical balancing act for Moley.

Part of this encouragement had to come from the executive, from him and his office. It could be rhetorical, but it also had to have something more. The new administration must seize the moment to act and act with dispatch. Perhaps above all else, the nation would want action. Four months of congressional and executive delay could be used to their rhetorical and legislative advantage.

Roosevelt then turned to Lincoln. He had used his presidential authority in unprecedented ways. Roosevelt, too, would need to create the impression of firmness and resolve—in a word, leadership. He knew that the suffering nation would not abide a Seventy-third Congress that would continue to play politics with the country's misery. He must use this impatience to his advantage; times of crisis demanded bold, swift, decisive actions. Moley felt good about this: Berle already was working on a comprehensive legislative plan of action for either a special session or the regular session of the new Congress.

The final thing Roosevelt emphasized was precedent. Specifically, he reminded Moley that part of the reassurance they could offer the people was not premised on hopeful promises but on past triumphs. The American people had a strong, proud tradition; he must evoke it to catalyze the country toward rapid, constructive action.

Roosevelt made no mention of the Providential or the Divine. Neither did Moley.

Moley glanced at his watch; it was nearly 2 A.M. They had had an amazingly brief three hours of uninterrupted conversation. He reminded Roosevelt that they faced another long day. Then again, perhaps he said it more for himself than for the candidate. Clearly, Roosevelt was energized by the hubbub. More than anything else, Roosevelt seemed to draw energy from the company of others.

As Moley rose to take his leave, he gently admonished Roosevelt to get some rest. After all, Warren G. Harding might have taken his last breath in this very room at the Palace Hotel. Gallows humor did not seem to bother the candidate, especially when it came to matters of health and sickness. "All right," he said. "Go to bed, go to bed, you Jeremiah, and I'll read the newspapers until I get sleepy."

Raymond Moley headed back down the hallway. The inaugural address was now in his hands. Five months removed from March, it was not yet a burden. It was the highest honor.

CHAPTER THREE

November 8, 1932

Franklin Roosevelt's prophecy in the wee hours of September 23 at the Palace Hotel in San Francisco proved accurate to a degree that even he could not have imagined. His margin of victory in the popular vote would total an impressive 7 million. His electoral margin of 472–59 (forty-two states to Hoover's six) was much more impressive. In four very short years, Herbert Hoover had gone from a technocratic super-man to an out-of-touch misanthrope, from a forward-looking activist to a do-nothing conservative. The publicity that had built him up to inestimable heights in the summer and fall of 1928 had, by 1932, taken him to lows from which he had never fully recovered. He deserved neither.

On the evening of Tuesday, November 8, however, Ray Moley had no idea just how big the victory would be. He knew Roosevelt would win; even the grim pessimist Louis Howe had some inkling that the nation would not turn again to the stolid Hoover. Not when they had before them the thick-shouldered optimist with the well-worn fedora, the dramatic naval cape, the toothy grin, and always the upward jut of the jaw—a man who promised "bold, persistent experimentation" and a "new deal for the American people." This man was eminently likable. This was perhaps the fundamental reason Ray Moley had so readily volunteered his services back in January.

As the returns slowly came rolling in from across the country, the candidate and his staff mingled easily in the ballroom of New York City's Biltmore Hotel. They looked extremely favorable. They soothed Moley considerably, whose own demons seemed occasionally to eat away at the professor's outward confidence. Just fifteen days earlier, he had had a near panic attack in Warm Springs, Georgia. At 5:30 in the morning, unable to sleep, Moley sat down to sort things out with his trusty legal pad and pen. "Everyone tired," he began. "F.D.R. tired. Public tired."[1] He was near exhaustion, still coordinating policy and speeches on a second train trip through the Midwest and South. "Solution is in shortness from now on," he wrote as a reminder.

The doubt, the "hell of a responsibility" he had told Nell about, seemed to surround him in the chilly Georgia darkness. "The danger is that the speeches from now will show marks of 1. Tiredness. 2. my own confusion of mind—as to lack of confidence." Earlier in the campaign, Hoover, in his one memorable line, had labeled his opponent a "chameleon on scotch plaid." Now Moley's "confusion of mind" could destroy his candidate: "the chameleon tearing itself to pieces." Even the cheers that attended the candidate wherever he ventured did not seem to comfort the morose professor: "The reaction in the crowds immediately to be heard not important." Fortunately, they had only one more day aboard the Roosevelt Special. Any longer, and the ability to sort things out might fall victim to the omnivorous maw of the campaign.

Tonight, he would be done—save for one thing: the inaugural address. That would take some time, but he figured to have plenty of it, almost four months worth. Surely, he could write a compelling speech in the tranquility that the interregnum would bring. He had not written a word yet, but he had not yet had the time or the mental energy. But this was not the night to begin worrying about high-minded speeches or campaign-related duties. Tonight was a night for celebrating a job well done.

Shortly after midnight, Hoover sent his telegram of concession: "I congratulate you on the opportunity that has come to you to be of service to the country and I wish for you a most successful administration. In the common purpose of all of us I shall dedicate myself to every possible helpful effort. Herbert Hoover."[2] It was a nice note, but thoroughly Hooverian: formal, stiff, and a bit tedious on the ears and tongue. Roosevelt and Moley would also learn that it was wholly disingenuous.

It was precisely this fact, above all others, that would take the professor once again out of the classroom and into Roosevelt's inner sanctum.

The telegram did seem to have one salutary effect: It brought Louis Howe out of his hiding from across the street, where he had been fretting and sweating the vote totals at campaign headquarters. With Hoover's concession, it now seemed safe. The twenty-year plan to get "The Boss," as Howe called him, into the White House had come to fruition. Moley looked on with just a bit of self awareness as the president-elect distributed kudos: "There are two people in the United States more than anybody else who are responsible for this great victory. One is my old friend and associate, Colonel Louis McHenry Howe, and the other is that splendid American, Jim Farley."[3]

Doubtless, true. And Moley certainly could not begrudge Howe and Farley their just due. But why not "three" people?

Herbert Hoover was not the only one engaged in a bit of artifice on November 8. Eleanor Roosevelt was trying to put up a brave front, but many around her could detect the ambivalence that had been her steady companion since at least June. One of the most profound ironies of Eleanor's life had come full circle with her husband's election: What she had desperately hoped to avoid, she had actually helped to set in motion.

In the ballroom that evening was a young reporter from the *Chicago Tribune,* John Boettiger, who in time was to become her daughter Anna Roosevelt Dall's second husband. He sensed that amid all the pomp and circumstance in the Biltmore was a profoundly sad woman. "I wish I knew what you are really thinking and feeling," he asked the next First Lady.[4] Eleanor reported being "happy for my husband, . . . But for myself, I was probably more deeply troubled than even John Boettiger realized. As I saw it, this meant the end of any personal life of my own. . . . The turmoil in my heart and mind was rather great that night." The woman who for more than eleven years had cultivated a fierce independence saw the White House as a prison for her own enormous ambitions. She also knew something of what it meant to be First Lady: Her Aunt Edith—Mrs. Theodore Roosevelt—had occupied the position for nearly two full terms. "I cannot say that I was pleased at the prospect."

Eleanor was equally blue about her new role the following day. On Wednesday, she invited Associated Press writer and soon-to-be intimate friend Lorena "Hick" Hickok to attend the classes that Eleanor taught at the all-girls private school, Todhunter, of which she was part proprietor. In the current-events class for senior girls, they discussed such issues as "What makes people commit suicide?" Eleanor's unhappiness no doubt contributed to the class' conversation.

While Eleanor had long since gotten over the point where she allowed her emotional distresses to effect her physical well-being, she had apparently given some thought to escaping what had looked in July like a possibility, but with her husband's election had become a reality. According to three of her closest friends—Nancy Cook, Marion Dickerman, and her rumored paramour and bodyguard Earl Miller—she sent a note along with Cook to the nominating convention in Chicago. With Roosevelt's fourth ballot victory, Cook panicked and showed the letter to Louis Howe. He promptly shredded it and warned Cook and Dickerman: "You are not to breathe a word of this to anyone. Not to *anyone*."[5]

There was a very simple reason for Howe's extreme reaction: Eleanor stated emphatically in the letter that she could not bear to become First Lady. She would rather run away and marry Earl Miller!

Howe had heard the talk of divorce before. In fact, he helped to keep the couple together in the devastating aftermath of the discovery of Franklin's 1918 affair with Eleanor's social secretary, Lucy Mercer. After discovering a packet of love letters as she unpacked her husband's bags upon his return from Europe and the war, Eleanor offered him his independence. Franklin refused. Politically and otherwise, he could not afford it. Fourteen years later, it was Eleanor who again apparently broached the subject. To what extent, if any, Howe again mediated is unknown. To what extent, if any, her husband even knew of her reaction to his penultimate victory is also unknown.

The next day, Eleanor was on a plane with her husband, bravely enduring eight hours worth of strong headwinds and a weak stomach. Howe met the couple at the airport in Chicago. Was he there to put out marital fires or only to foist upon Franklin his version of the acceptance speech? Perhaps both.

Back at Todhunter, Eleanor gave "Hick" some very forthright "on-the-record" statements: "I never wanted to be a President's wife, and I don't want it now. You don't quite believe me, do you? Very likely no one would—except possibly some woman who had had the job."[6] Once again she would again have "to work out my own salvation."

And yet, was it not Eleanor who had played such a pivotal part in making her husband president? Was it not Eleanor who had bravely nursed him in the depths of his darkest hours, when his body was being ravaged by the polio virus? Was it not Eleanor who had prevailed against her overbearing mother-in-law, Sara Roosevelt, when it came to Franklin's future? She had understood that her husband's soul would whither and die, just like his legs, should his future consist only of looking after the family's Hyde Park estate. Politics was his lifeblood; it kept him yearning to get to the end of the driveway on his crutches; it brought people to him; it gave him something to live for. So she had helped him get it. She joined political organizations. Even though she was initially a terrible public speaker, woefully lacking in confidence, she stumped all over the state just to keep his name on the voters' lips and in the newspapers. Louis Howe taught her how to deal with the press and how to give a political speech. Her husband offered his advice on the mechanics of politics.

Eleanor was obedient. She had done her duties only too well. Her husband's highest aspirations had become a reality.

What had she done? Who was she now? What would become of her?

Fortunately for Eleanor, she had something to fall back on, since working out her "salvation" was nothing new for her.

During her husband's days in the Wilson administration, she had been forced to learn the District's political and social culture. Unlike her ambitious husband, she did not particularly like the culture. She was raising five young children in a new city; she was attempting to juggle the logistics for households in New York City, Hyde Park, Campobello Island, and Washington, D. C.; she was frequently abandoned by her husband, the hobnobbing assistant secretary of the navy; and always she was negotiating turf with her interloping mother-in-law. After the devastation of the Lucy Mercer affair, even the family pictures changed. Looking emaciated and gaunt from the trauma, Eleanor could not bring herself to meet the camera's gaze. She looked down, staring inconsolably at nothing. She had been abandoned.

Eleanor's reaction to the election returns thus was not solely about the corseted constraints of being First Lady. That was merely about playing a role, albeit a public one. The emotional cartography of the capital was another matter; her unhappiest moments as a woman had been experienced there. In a city teeming with people and power, she had been alone in her grief. Except for one inanimate, perhaps maudlin, source of companionship.

In the days and months following the discovery of her husband's marital infidelities, Eleanor would seek tranquility and strength in a most unusual place: Rock Creek Cemetery. Several times a week she would drive the not-insignificant distance from the Roosevelt's commodious N Street home to the graveyard. There she would often sit for hours, drawing inspiration from a nameless monument.

At the center of the cemetery's meadow, enclosed by holly, was a small sanctuary containing a formidable statue designed by the famed sculptor Augustus Saint-Gaudens. It was a monument to the wife of a famous man. Profoundly depressed over her husband's infidelities, she had killed herself by drinking photographic acid at the age of forty-two.

During the Lincoln era in Washington, D. C., social circles claimed that no more "modern" woman existed than Marian Sturgis (né Hooper) Adams. Educated in Greek, Latin, and the modern languages at the Agassiz school for girls in Cambridge, Marian, or "Clover" as she was known, married the famed American historian Henry Adams in 1872. Their home, directly across from the White House in Lafayette Square, soon became ground zero for entertainment among the capital's political and intellectual elite.

Clover Adams, though, had skills that far transcended throwing glamorous soirees in her home. She was a patient researcher and a translator of note. Much of her work ended up in her husband's scholarship. But Henry Adams was no admirer of womens' minds or their intellectual ambitions. He wrote of the "pathetic impossibility" that women could actually improve their "poor little hard, thin, wiry, one-stringed instruments which they call their minds."[7] Seeking her own creative outlets, Clover turned to photographic studies—with no small success. But when her portraits brought admirers, Henry Adams prohibited their sale.

He also had admirers of his own, including the most beautiful woman in Washington, Elizabeth Cameron, wife of Sen. William Don Cameron. The two developed a deep and abiding love for one another. The Washington socialite set claimed that not long after Clover found out about her husband's infidelities, she fell into a deep depression. On December 6, 1885, she ingested the chemicals of her avocation and died.

Adams's grief, if he bore any, was sublimated in the most curious of ways: total effacement. He never mentioned his wife in public again; he never mentioned her or their marriage in any of his writings; he destroyed every letter sent to her; and he destroyed much of her photographic and intellectual work. But he did commission Saint-Gaudens to build a life-size bronze statue that Adams called "Peace of God." Eleanor Roosevelt referred to the hooded, robed figure simply as "Grief."

The monument bore no explicit reference to Clover Adams; she would be nameless in death.

Eleanor obviously felt a deep, abiding kinship with Saint-Gaudens's figure. No doubt she also felt a certain kinship with the vicissitudes born by Clover Adams. But she did not, and would not, succumb to them. Lucy Mercer would not be to her what Elizabeth Cameron had been to Clover Adams. Rather, she would draw no small measure of strength from the solitary statue in the enclosed holly garden where she would often sit by herself for hours.

"Grief" had become so important to Eleanor, such a part of her living fiber, that she carried its visage with her—not just in memory, but also textually. Never far from her was a poem written about "Grief" by Cecil Spring-Rice.

O steadfast, deep, inexorable eyes
Set look inscrutable, nor smile nor frown!
O tranquil eyes that look so calmly down
Upon a world of passion and lies![8]

On the night her husband called "the greatest night of my life," the night she learned she would once again return to the city of her earlier heartache, perhaps she was momentarily comforted by the memory of "Grief," and the stoicism of its implacable gaze.[9] She would again seek the statue out in the hours before her husband's inaugural address.

She might also have been comforted that same evening by that most uncomforting looking creature, Louis Howe; it would not have been the first time. She could tell the gnomish, ashen, and asthmatic newspaperman almost anything—even her impending elopement with her bodyguard! And Howe no doubt could read her much the same way he had learned to read her husbands many moods.

Howe had mediated crises between the two before, notably the Lucy Mercer contretemps. He had convinced both that each needed the other. But he also knew something of Eleanor's darkness, her insecurities, and her abiding fear of Washington and the presidency. No doubt, he had accompanied her to "Grief." No doubt, she had spoken of its importance to him.

Despite the image of being a hard-boiled newspaperman with a chip on his slight shoulder, Howe was something of an artist. He dabbled in watercolors and the stage. He also occasionally wrote verse, though more often than not it was the doggerel of campaign rumor and innuendo, meant to amuse The Boss. By 1932, Howe had worked continuously for nearly twenty years with one single ambition: to get Franklin Roosevelt elected president. As this ambition was transformed from inchoate planning into political reality, he was attuned to Eleanor's sorrows and fears. He sent her two poems, both of which resonate deeply with the statue in the sequestered holly grove at Rock Creek Cemetery. In a three-stanza poem titled "A Question," Howe asked a question, couched in the symbol of death:

Grim and silent—row on row
Stand the gravestones white with snow
Summers come and summers go
But they neither heed nor know
—Like the dead that lie below

Ye who rest beneath each stone
All so utterly alone
Now life's bitter jest is shown
Did your happy hours atone
For the suffering you have known?

Long forgotten have ye lain
Would you live your lives again
Knowing all your striving vain—
That to mark your toil and pain
Only tombstones now remain?[10]

A question, yes—two, in fact. And given to a woman fixated with a gravestone, Howe's poem surely had an interested audience. Was this an invocation of the memory of Clover Adams, who knew something of "bitter jest" and suffering and loneliness—and whose memorial served as a beacon for Eleanor's sorrows? Was this less of a question and more of a direct challenge to a woman confronted with yet more suffering, pain, and toil on the immediate horizon? In this metaphysical battle between happiness and sorrow, living in happiness or being dead to the pain that living brings, was not Eleanor willing to forsake a "grim and silent" eternity for a few "happy hours" of living? Howe had overdetermined her choice. Why did he need to?

Less than a month later, on the first day of the year that would see his boss claim the ultimate political prize, Howe gave Eleanor a second poem. It, too, bore vestiges of "Grief." And it, too, suggested a better future again premised on a fateful choice:

We are the hooded brotherhood of fears
Barring the pleasant path that lay ahead
Who, grim and silent, all these futile years
Have filled your timid soul with numbing
  dread

And though you sought to lag behind
And though you sought some other road
Ever before you would you find
Our shrouded, brotherhood still strode

Fool! Had you dared to speed your pace
Our masking cowles aside to tear
And meet us bravely face to face
We would have vanished into air.[11]

The "brotherhood of fears," of course, was a construction, a figment of Eleanor's imagination. The path to the future was blocked only in her mind. Just as the "Grim and silent" of "A Question" stood for death, so too did the "grim and silent" brotherhood of fears. It was a death to possibility, a death that Louis Howe desperately hoped Eleanor would confront face-to-face.

She sealed each poem carefully in protective coverings.

Fear and death: the two were intimately related.

Eleanor's fears blocked the future; the immaterial was killing off all that could be.

The only thing that Eleanor had to fear was, well, fear itself.

CHAPTER FOUR

November 22, 1932

The end was finally in sight for Raymond Moley. While he had odds
and ends to clean up, the last major assignment was now coming into
view. It was an assignment he welcomed. Compared to the frenzy of
the campaign and all of the Democratic politicians trying to get a piece
of the candidate, the inaugural address would be an enjoyable task. He
had not yet started writing, but the ideas from the Palace Hotel conversation were still percolating. Perhaps more importantly, a committee would not be assembling this speech. From beginning to end, it
would belong to Roosevelt and not the fragmented constituencies that
had taxed Moley's inventional skills, and occasionally his patience,
during the fall campaign.

On the evening of Wednesday, November 9, Moley headed back to
his apartment and immediately fell into a "dreamlike repose."[1] He met
his classes at Columbia. He smoked his pipe. He listened to the quiet
that now enveloped him and tried to put some of his own closure on
the headiest adventure of his life. It might also keep him in good graces
with the future president. On Saturday, November 12, Moley worked
up a semiformal note of congratulations to the man closest to Roosevelt.
He borrowed from the president-elect's store of playful names: this
would be the one time where he would address him as "Colonel" Louis
McHenry Howe. "It is not given to many to know the realization of
their dreams," Moley intoned. "You are one of the chosen few for whom

the dream lived in the morning after." He was, of course, not unaware of the intricate network of loyalties that enabled him to have access to Roosevelt: "the place I enjoyed in this campaign is due to the fact that you and I have been friends a long time." Moley was exaggerating: He had been close to Howe really for less than a year—but he had seen firsthand just how jealous Howe could be toward those who had trespassed in territory that he assiduously monitored and policed. Moley continued where Roosevelt had left off during election night at the Biltmore: "You and Jim [Farley] have done more than elect a President. You have created a new party that ought to hold power for twenty five years."[2] Even while he was playing prophet with no small measure of perspicacity, Moley could not have known just how important being in Louis Howe's good graces would be over the course of the next four months.

While Moley was finishing his letter/paean to Howe, Herbert Hoover was also engaged in important letter writing meant to curry favor. Like Moley, he, too, probably entertained motives beyond what the letter might have said. That letter would also link Ray Moley to him. It would also function to link Moley to his erstwhile boss in ways that the professor probably never considered. The lengthy telegram was sent on November 12 as the president's train stopped in San Bernadino, California, on the way back to Washington, D. C. It was not a note of congratulations; rather, it was a lengthy discourse on foreign war debts.

Hoover, as was his penchant, had very clear ideas about how to proceed. He needed congressional help for any negotiations of the foreign debt, and he would need Roosevelt's assistance with a lame-duck Congress that was very hostile to him. He did not mince words: "if there is to be any change in the attitude of the Congress it will be greatly affected by the views of those members who recognize you as their leader and who will properly desire your counsel and advice." Hoover therefore requested the "opportunity to confer with you personally at some convenient date in the near future." He would "be only too glad to have you bring into this conference any of the Democratic Congressional leaders or other advisers you may wish."[3]

The telegram was received early Sunday morning, November 13, in Albany.

Ray Moley's "interlude of infinite peace" was over after just three days. He would be Roosevelt's "other" adviser. He did not yet know that, however.

Moley helped to formulate Roosevelt's response to the telegram. He did not need to do too much reading between the lines to see just what Hoover was up to: He was attempting to line up Roosevelt's support for how he proposed to solve the terribly volatile problem of foreign debts.

Moley confessed amazement at the temerity of the president's proposal: He was attempting to use the issue of foreign debts to leverage Roosevelt into agreeing with a fundamental principle of the Hooverian orthodoxy: the depression had its origins abroad. Roosevelt's reply to Hoover's telegram was cordial, but tepid: "I am glad to cooperate in every appropriate way, subject, of course, to the requirements of my present duties as Governor of this state." Furthermore, Roosevelt would be "delighted" to call on Hoover at the White House just as soon as he had gotten over his postelection cold. Roosevelt added a seemingly innocent suggestion: Would the president mind if "we make this meeting wholly informal and personal. You and I can go over the entire situation." This was Roosevelt's preferred mode of communication—interpersonal—where he could be just as expansive and as agreeable as possible, minus hard and fast commitments to policy. But however Hoover wanted to plan the arrangements—and because he was still president, Roosevelt had to appear deferential to the office, not necessarily to the man—he gave strong indications how he felt about the president's coercive internationalism: "in the last analysis, the immediate question raised by the British, French and other notes creates a responsibility which now rests upon those now vested with executive and legislative authority."[4] Hoover, not Roosevelt, was in charge—as he would be for the next four months. Moley seemed pleased with this final sentiment; after all, had not their entire campaign emphasis been on domestic problems and domestic solutions? Why abandon what had clearly resonated with the voters? Why abandon the nascent New Deal before it even started? Moley already was in possession of Berle's five-page memo written on November 10 that outlined a very ambitious legislative program premised on the assumption that economic recovery was a domestic issue, not an international one.

Had Herbert Hoover responded favorably to Roosevelt's suggestion of a "wholly informal" meeting, Ray Moley's life might have taken a very different, perhaps much more anonymous, turn. Instead, Hoover decided to press the issue of getting Roosevelt's assent to his plans. And so, on November 17, the president telephoned the president-elect about their upcoming meeting: it would not be "wholly informal." Said Hoover: "I have a number of things I would like to discuss with you, and I wonder if you could bring someone with you. Because there are a lot of things [that] ought to be looked into which cannot be decided on the minute. A secretary or somebody."[5] The statement was loaded with assumptions—not the least of which was that Hoover and Roosevelt actually had policy options on which to base decisions. Roosevelt responded: "Yes, I can bring a secretary. I hadn't thought of anybody." Hoover then shifted the dialogue to a different, more consequential level. "I would like to bring in Ogden Mills because I would like to give you an outline of what is going on abroad, and I wonder if there is someone you could bring along." With the mention of Ogden Mills, Hoover had raised the stakes of their impending meeting considerably.

Mills was formidable and Roosevelt knew it. He was so formidable that he and Moley had agreed during the campaign not to make much over the issue of international finance for fear of having to parry with Mills, Hoover's treasury secretary and Roosevelt's Hyde Park neighbor. Clearly, no mere secretary on the order of a Missy LeHand, a Marvin McIntyre, or even a Louis Howe would do.

Later that day, Hoover issued a brief, five-sentence announcement. The president-elect would join him for an "informal" meeting late in the afternoon on Tuesday, November 22. "The President will be accompanied by Secretary Mills. Governor Roosevelt will be accompanied by someone interested in the subject."[6] The White House correspondents might have gotten a good chuckle out of this last patronizing sentence.

Presumably, "someone" from among Roosevelt's inner circle might be "interested" in matters of international finance.

Hoover did not know whom.

Roosevelt, during the phone conversation, did not know whom, either.

Later that same day, Moley arrived back in Albany. He was informed that evening that he would be accompanying the president-elect to the meeting. For the second time in four days, Moley's plans had been waylaid: He would be the "someone" who was "interested" in the manifold complexities of international finance.

He was stunned at the news. Moreover, he had not even been asked. Roosevelt's appointments secretary had merely informed him that he would be accompanying Roosevelt to Washington, D.C., on November 22. The meeting, Moley knew, would forever change his life. No longer would his existence in political affairs be relatively anonymous. More importantly, just as he had noted back in April, this would be a "terrifying responsibility." He had all of four days to prepare himself and Roosevelt for a "conference"—not even a meeting anymore, as the press was to report—with the two men who knew more about the foreign debt as it related to the country's economic policy than anyone else alive.

Raymond Moley had good reason to be terrified.

The four men seemed to smoke just a bit too exuberantly. The president worked on a thick-ringed Cuban cigar, while Mills, Moley, and Roosevelt opted for the cigarettes that had been laid out in advance. The president seemed uneasy, nervous. Roosevelt was also nervous, but he attempted to diffuse the tension with a crack directed at Mills, something about a Republican National Committee ad that had confused the two of them as it related to ownership of a private golf course.

Hoover was not in a joking mood.

He launched into a detailed, one-hour lecture on the war debt. Instead of directing his attention to his soon-to-be successor, he alternated between looking at Moley and staring at the seal of the United States that had been woven into the Red Room's thick carpet. The crux of the debate involved the possible default on a loan payment by the British, French, Italians, and Greeks scheduled for December 15. What would happen to international markets if the countries did not meet their financial obligations? Cancellation of the debt was not an option for Hoover, and default would have economic consequences at home. His favored position was that each of the countries should be given the opportunity to reexamine or renegotiate its debt obligations to the United States. But this would require congressional approval, something he could not get—by himself, anyway.

Roosevelt asked some questions on three-by-five-inch cards that Moley had prepared. Mills and Hoover alternately answered. The solution Hoover proposed—and hence the reason for the meeting—was a jointly reconstituted Debt Commission. He and Roosevelt would select members such that there could be continuity once the new administration assumed control on March 4. Hoover seemed to have backed Roosevelt into a corner, since the president-elect had agreed that debtors should indeed have access to their creditors.

Roosevelt turned to Moley and asked, "Don't you think so, Ray?"[7]

This was clearly a plea for help. Moley responded that, yes, creditors should grant such access, to which Roosevelt responded, "Well, then, where do we go from there?"

Moley quickly realized that Roosevelt was getting a bit desperate for some rhetorical assistance. From the professor's vantage point, the very possibility of the New Deal seemed to hang in the balance. Moley boldly put forward his/Roosevelt's views to the two best minds in the country on the issue.

He was against the idea of a Debt Commission—jointly reconstituted or not. The press would parlay a commission into new fears about the debt situation, thereby exacerbating, not alleviating, economic uncertainty—the bane of banks and businesses. Moreover, Moley knew that the lame-duck Seventy-second Congress was hostile to debt revision and certainly debt cancellation. For Roosevelt to be on the losing side of an international debt battle before he even entered office would spell potential disaster for the new administration's ambitious reform plans. The New Deal would be stillborn, suffocated by congressional and popular reluctance to spend so much precious time on negotiations that might never come to pass.

No, Moley was firmly against a Debt Commission. He was forcefully in favor, though, of using all available diplomatic channels—most notably the State Department—to enable debtor nations to get a fair hearing on their ability to pay. Moley was improvising now, but Roosevelt fell in quickly with this line of thinking.

The professor's diagnosis on debts did not sit well with the president or his treasury secretary. He had desperately wanted Roosevelt's assent; instead, he had gotten some neophyte political scientist's ruminations on international economic diplomacy.

Moley noticed that his suggestions had transformed the nervous tension into unmistakable hostility. There was no loud swearing, no hostile interrogations, no table pounding. The air, nevertheless, was thick with distrust and anger.

As the afternoon wore on, and as it became clear that Roosevelt would not be persuaded to go along with a Debt Commission, Hoover wrote up a very brief, vague note for the papers. "The President and Governor Roosevelt traversed at length the subjects mentioned in their telegraphic communication. It is felt that progress has been made."[8] The "it" who was feeling that progress had been made was not specified. Yet, progress between the two parties had in a way been made: It just was not a progress leading to cooperation. It was a progress of articulating differences. It was exactly the type of progress that Hoover had hoped to avoid.

The meeting ended with the agreement that both sides would issue separate policy statements. Hoover figured to have the upper hand in the stakes for public opinion. Moreover, the press and the public would be able to judge for themselves just how uncooperative the president-elect was being. Two weeks had clearly not exhausted Hoover's animus over the election results. Perhaps he could get some measure of vindication during the interregnum.

That evening, back at the Mayflower Hotel, Bernard Baruch called on the professor, who proceeded to inform him of the afternoon's momentous proceedings. After his recounting, and sensing that Moley's stamina might have run its course, Baruch ordered his young charge, "Young fellow, see that bed. Well, don't you dare get into it until you have written down what happened this afternoon."⁹ Moley was learning quickly that to run in such circles was to be privy to, and part of, the historical record. He did Baruch one better: He decided to keep a diary. He would also keep a careful record of his work on the inaugural address. Who knew? It might be a historical speech even beyond the fact of its rare generic status.

In hindsight, what seemed to weigh heavily on Moley was how very different were these two protagonists in America's history. Where Roosevelt would disarm with good-natured ribbing, Hoover was awkwardly formal. Where Roosevelt would make policy seemingly by the seat of his pants, Hoover was implacable in his policy beliefs. Where Roosevelt was a master of masks, Hoover was largely incapable of disingenuous posturing. Here was a man who could govern only under the most favorable auspices.

Moley noticed that Hoover wore the convictions of his certainty. To disagree with him was to disagree with more than an idea, an opinion, a contingent formulation of policy. It was to disagree with a constellation of virtues. His was not a political mind; it was the mind of a diffident engineer cum evangelist.

And yet, there was something more profoundly personal in the president's barely concealed contempt for his successor. But for Herbert Hoover, the personal and the political constituted two sides of the same proverbial coin. His fifteen-year "relationship" with Franklin Roosevelt was a case in point.

During the halcyon days of the Wilson administration, both men had cut their political teeth on the great events of World War I and its aftermath. Hoover had become something of an international savior, having seen to it that millions of the Great War's innocents had periodic meals. He was also something of a postwar savant at the negotiating table. The English iconoclast, John Maynard Keynes, cast Hoover at the Versailles Treaty talks in near mythical terms: "Mr. Hoover was the only man who emerged from the ordeal of Paris with an enhanced reputation. This complex personality, with his habitual air of weary Titan" brought to the talks "precisely that atmosphere of reality, knowledge, magnanimity, and disinterestedness which, if they had been found in other quarters also, would have given us the Good Peace."[10]

He and his wife, Lou, were also occasional dinner guests of the Roosevelts. Likewise with Eleanor and her husband. The couples' social calendars indicate that they dined together at least eight times between March, 1917, and March, 1920. If they were not friends, these two young rising political stars were certainly friendly. Roosevelt, the somewhat green assistant secretary of the navy, was eight years Hoover's junior, but by 1920 he already had developed a keen eye for political talent. In a letter to the U.S. ambassador to Poland, Hugh Gibson, Roosevelt reported that he had been sizing up the millionaire mining engineer turned international goodwill ambassador as a possible political recruit: "I had some nice talks with Herbert Hoover before he went west for Christmas. He is certainly a wonder and I wish we could make him President of the United States. There could not be a better one."[11] Roosevelt's opinion would change significantly during the next twelve years, but in the winter of 1920, as the Democrats were casting around for an heir to the legacy of Woodrow Wilson, the still ideologically unaffiliated Hoover was being courted by Franklin Roosevelt. Perhaps ironically, Roosevelt would himself run as the Democratic vice presidential candidate later that year. Could he have envisioned a Hoover-Roosevelt ticket? If he had, he likely would have embraced it. But by 1931, Roosevelt was so embarrassed by his ardent support of a Hoover presidential candidacy that he told his campaign biographer to strike it from the historical record.

If the 1920s were Hoover's political high point, the era was Roosevelt's nadir—politically and personally. Hoover, as commerce secretary during the Harding-Coolidge presidencies, seemed to have a significant stake in seemingly countless government-business relationships. It was a job ideally suited to his political dispositions: he could organize, order, cajole, and publicize minus the concerns of electoral politics and public opinion. Hoover was not a traditional party man, and, as a result, his ambitions for the department were not constrained by party loyalties. So, for example, as part of his program for better business efficiency, he could enthusiastically approve the new president of the American Construction Council—none other than Franklin Roosevelt.

The former assistant navy secretary and failed vice-presidential candidate was eager and grateful for the appointment. Just nine months earlier, he had been badly crippled with infantile paralysis. Many figured his political ambitions were over. He would be an invalid, looked after by his doting mother, Sara. Presidential politics, surely, would not permit of crippled bodies.

From the summer of 1921 through the summer of 1928, Roosevelt spent the great bulk of his days relearning his own body, with the express purpose of learning how to walk again. Or, giving the appearance that he could walk. Learning—no, mastering—appearances would prove invaluable to his presidential ambitions. Out of politics physically for seven years, this would prove to be a most valuable apprenticeship. Meanwhile, Hoover's presidential ambitions were pursued in a more traditional fashion.

By the summer of 1927, his success and publicity at commerce, and his near-mythical reputation combined with Coolidge's intention not to seek the office, conspired to make Hoover the Republican Party's leading presidential candidate. It also precipitated the ending of cordial relations with Franklin Roosevelt, who had other political debts to pay.

By 1928, Roosevelt was deep in political debt to Al Smith, the New York governor and Democratic presidential nominee. Members of the Smith camp, with the active persuasion of Roosevelt loyalists, had asked the recovering paralytic to place Smith's name in nomination at the 1924 Democratic National Convention. It was a huge break for Roosevelt, who had been out of the political limelight for nearly three years. His speech, the "Happy Warrior" address, was far and away the high point of a dismal convention. It took the Democrats two weeks and 102 ballots to compromise on the nondescript John W. Davis as their presidential candidate. Roosevelt struggled to the podium on crutches to deliver his address. He had practiced the "walk" for weeks. The political comeback was officially under way.

Four years later, at the Democratic National Convention in Houston, Smith again asked Roosevelt to place his name in nomination. Again, Roosevelt accepted, although this time he walked to the podium without the aid of crutches. Using a technique that he had perfected while convalescing at Warm Springs, Georgia, Roosevelt—with the assistance of a stiff cane, a be-muscled arm, and rigid leg braces—gave the appearance of a man walking slowly, but perambulatory all the same. Instead of an invalid, the audience in Houston saw a man who was merely lame. He looked robust and ruddy, and that ringing Roosevelt tenor found its way into homes across the nation with another iteration of the Happy Warrior. Roosevelt might well have been speaking of himself.

It was in his capacity as an Al Smith partisan that relations between he and Hoover soured. It was also, likely, inadvertent.

A letter dated September 25, 1928, bearing Franklin Roosevelt's signature was sent to Hoover friend and ardent supporter, Julius Barnes. How Barnes ended up receiving a very pro-Smith letter is unknown. More troubling was that the letter was also very anti-Hoover. Under a Smith presidency, the letter detailed, "our country stands far more chance of returning to the path blazed out for us by our greatest President [Wilson], than under the materialistic and self-seeking advisors who surround the other candidate."[12] That Barnes was one such "advisor" did not help matters. But Roosevelt went even further, impugning Hoover for his "crass materialism" and a "dollar-and-cents viewpoint of everything."

It was a form letter. Chances are Roosevelt had not even signed it, let alone specified the address. But it was a dreadful political (and personal) boner—one that ended up in the hands of the next president, who had done Roosevelt no small favors during his seven years in the political wilderness. Hoover also tended to be thin-skinned, politically and otherwise. It was a slight that would be neither forgiven nor forgotten. Fifty months later, he still had difficulty looking Roosevelt in the eye.

One week after the ill-fated letter was sent, Roosevelt had acquiesced to the frequent and tenacious entreaties of Smith and key New York

Democrats. He would run for governor. He would run reluctantly, but eight years removed from public life, he would run. In the weeks leading up to the election, he "ran" all over the state, showing voters he was active, vigorous, and healthy. He won by the narrowest of margins, but he won; and, by dint of this victory, Franklin Roosevelt was thereafter considered presidential timbre.

Their relationship, or what was left of it, deteriorated rapidly. On April 13, 1929, a little more than a month after his inauguration, Hoover was lampooned at the annual meeting of the Gridiron Club. According to Hoover's guest and dinner companion, Edgar Rickard, he took the "club gibes in fine humor." All, that is, except for the gibes of New York's new governor. The president felt the "Roosevelt attack keenly and questions if his rebuke [was] in order."[13]

In the fall of 1930, with economic indicators continuing to spiral downward, Roosevelt ran for reelection less against the nominal Republican nominee, Charles Tuttle, than he did against the president. Throughout the campaign, Roosevelt hammered away at the lack of leadership in Washington and the administration's seemingly disingenuous claims that things would soon get better. "Nothing happened but words," Roosevelt would thunder, without irony. Early on, the governor had aptly noted that the Hooverian response to what would be called the Great Depression was to persuade people that better days were soon ahead. It was an immaterial economics: belief, not legislation, was the sine qua non of economic recovery.

A smart political response on Hoover's part would have been to ignore the Empire State upstart. Let the governor rail against the administration; as president, he had much bigger fish to fry. But Hoover's thin skin again got in the way of smart politics. And so, in late October, the president dispatched several of his administration's "heavies" to New York State, including the very weighty secretary of state, Henry Stimson. Also sent to New York to campaign against Roosevelt was the governor's Hyde Park neighbor, Ogden Mills.

Roosevelt loved the attention, even flaunting it. Here was presidential-caliber publicity that he could never hope to buy. Things only got better/bitter with Roosevelt's tally on Election Day: He won by the unprecedented plurality of 725,000 votes. It was a staggering sum, more than twice the total that the popular Smith had received in his best year. The day after the votes had been tallied, Will Rogers stated without humor that the Democrats had nominated their president.

The nation did not know it. Even many of his closest advisers did not know it. But Herbert Hoover was buoyed by the news of a Roosevelt presidential candidacy. It was not the last time the president would badly underestimate the crippled governor.

The fact of her husband's crippled condition always weighed heavily on Eleanor Roosevelt, but never more so than when he was forced to do political things in person in public. She knew that any misstep, any fall might mean the end of the deception and the end of her husband's presidential aspirations. She also knew that he needed to attend to politics in the public eye, if for no other reason than to quell the rampant whisperings about his fragile health. The whispering had practically followed her husband home from the hospital in October, 1921. Throughout his lengthy convalescence, she had heard that her husband was too sick to hold elected office, particularly as a chief executive. How could a man lead when he could not even walk without help? Had he not suffered a paralytic stroke that had affected his brain? Or had her husband perhaps contracted syphilis? The rumors were rampant, and they seemed to reach a fever pitch with each new election. She knew 1932 would be no different, but she did not think Herbert Hoover would try to make political capital out of them.

Eleanor had accompanied her husband to the twenty-fourth annual Governors' Conference, which was meeting in late April in Richmond, Virginia. It had been unseasonably hot. Her husband was the frontrunner for the Democratic presidential nomination, and she understood that governors—both Republican and Democrat—would be taking the bodily measure of Franklin. She had not thought, though, that the president might do the same. That afternoon, she had felt sorry for the president, for as he was addressing the assembled delegation— a speech that was being broadcast live to the nation—a gust of wind blew away his papers, scattering them all over. He had been so reliant on his prepared text that he had to stop his speech then and there. It had been an awkward moment, especially for those in the immediate audience.

That evening, however, her husband came under the microscope. The governors and their wives had been invited by the Hoovers to dine at the White House. Eleanor was aware of the protocol: She and her husband would have to stand and wait in the East Room until the president and First Lady received them. She and Franklin arrived early, as they often did for such events, since he preferred to walk rather than be pushed in his wheelchair. They assumed their place in the East Room and then waited.

And waited.

Twenty minutes had passed and her husband was perspiring mightily from the exertion and the hot, humid weather. He was offered a chair. Twice. Twice he refused. He had something to prove to the other governors.

Both Eleanor's and her husband's minds raced: How could the president make cruel political sport out of his disability? His lateness surely was meant to show up the Democratic frontrunner. Finally, a full half-hour late, Herbert and Lou Hoover met their assembled dinner guests. Franklin half collapsed into a nearby chair. Neither he nor his wife would forgive the president for putting him through this cruel test.[14]

Hoover, though, had no intentions of showing up his main rival. To think that he would purposefully try to make light of Roosevelt's disability, he later wrote, was absurd. He was above such base political motives. In the spring of 1932, Hoover had other motives when it came to his principal challenger. The president definitely did not want the assembled governors to see Roosevelt in such physical peril. If anything, Hoover wanted Roosevelt to put his best foot forward, so to speak. More succinctly, he wanted Roosevelt to win his party's nomination. Badly. His own electoral prospects, he figured, hung in the balance. His reasoning was premised on both mental and physical considerations.

As early as February, 1932, Hoover and his press secretary, Theodore Joslin, were strategizing for November. Both men were elated that Al Smith had decided to enter the Democratic race; it would make for a tough fight. On February 7, Joslin recorded in his diary what would be the private line adopted by the White House: "I would prefer Roosevelt to almost any other leading Democrat for the President's opponent, for the people would come to understand he has not the ability nor the mentality to be President."[15] As if to clarify the point about "ability," Joslin continued, "As an unfortunate fact, too, he is a paralytic, depriving him of the physical strength properly to handle the duties of President." That this view was not Joslin's alone is attested to by what he recorded on the evening of April 27, the evening that Franklin and Eleanor dined at the White House.

Joslin, Hoover, and Walter Newton, Hoover's personal secretary, huddled together after the governors left. "We discussed the elections in Mass and Pennsylvania, with the President strongly of the opinion the results meant the elimination of Roosevelt." But if these losses were not enough, there was always the matter of Roosevelt's health. "He shouldn't think of running. He is a sick man. He wouldn't live a year in the White House." Hoover had no doubt seen the governor laboring just to stand that evening. He had also been privy to the commotion caused by Roosevelt's near collapse into a chair. But the nation had not seen Roosevelt struggling just to stand. Nor had they seen the Democratic frontrunner struggling to get out of his automobile that evening. But Hoover had, and he noted how newspaper photographers had been prevented from getting unflattering photos of him. Roosevelt had strategically employed a phalanx of aides, who gathered around him as he was moved from his car to a standing position. This complex maneuver had been conducted with such aplomb that Hoover figured the voters would never find out just how disabled the governor truly was.[16]

However, the fact of Roosevelt's lameness aside, Hoover desperately wanted him as his opponent come the general election because he simply was not presidential material. Political aides and elite opinion had it that the governor was, as one family member put it, something of a "feather duster." The venerable Walter Lippmann had publicly disparaged Roosevelt as "a pleasant man, who without any important qualifications for the office would very much like to be president."[17]

In May, the running conversation about a Roosevelt candidacy between Hoover and Joslin continued. The president was deflated by Roosevelt's defeat in the California primary: "'This just about ends Roosevelt. He can't get the Democratic nomination now and I am sorry.'" Joslin figured otherwise, and tried to reassure the president: "I have been saying for some weeks that the Democrats are practically certain to nominate Governor Roosevelt. The President asked me today if I had changed my mind. 'Not at all,' I replied. 'Nothing has happened to change the situation.'" Hoover was less sanguine. "'Well I hope you are right,' he said, 'but I think you are wrong. I hate to think it, but I believe they will nominate Newton Baker.'"

Two weeks later, in late June, commenting on anti-Roosevelt remarks made by Frank Hague, Hoover told Joslin, "'It looks bad for Franklin. . . . Now if Roosevelt had any boldness in him he could get control of the situation [a controversy over a voting procedure at the convention] and ensure his nomination. . . . But he hasn't it in him. He is a trimmer, not a constructive leader.'" Hoover privately expressed to Joslin his fears that the Democrats meeting in Chicago would nominate the formidable Newton Baker, Wilson's secretary of war. "'I am afraid of Baker,' the president said. 'He's a strong second choice of the convention and would be a much harder man for me to beat.'" Joslin thought the president looked worried as he asked, "'Do you still think Roosevelt will be nominated?'" Joslin replied, "'Absolutely. He'll get it on the second or third ballot.'" The president nodded and said, "'I hope so. Our salvation lies largely in his nomination.'"

On Friday, July 1, Joslin was tipped off that McAdoo would release the California delegates to Roosevelt. He immediately sent an usher to tell Hoover, who was dining. The usher phoned Joslin and said, "the President smiled more broadly than he had in months when he received the message."

It had all gone exactly according to plan: On the fourth ballot, the Democrats had their man. So, too, did Herbert Hoover.

And so, as Ray Moley scribbled away in his suite at the Mayflower Hotel on the evening of November 22, he could not explain what he had witnessed. Why did Hoover display such contempt for the president-elect?

Why would he not even pay him the courtesy of occasional eye contact? Why the palpable distrust and suspicion? He could only surmise that Hoover still seethed over his November 8 loss. No doubt he did. But what Ray Moley did not know, could not have known, was the extent to which Hoover's own careful plans had been foiled by the crippled candidate with the lightweight intellect. Hoover hated to lose—especially to an inferior opponent—and he had lost badly.

But the game was not yet over.

CHAPTER FIVE

February 12–13, 1933

There was another game going on, and it had nothing to do with Herbert Hoover. It was a game for Raymond Moley's allegiances, and so far, Franklin Roosevelt had played it with a deft touch. In theory, Roosevelt could have brought anyone with him to consult with Hoover and Mills. Why not the two other Brain Trusters, Rex Tugwell or Adolph Berle? After all, they were the experts when it came to economics and finance. Moley's bailiwick was criminology and the courts, not the arcane and obscure ways and means of international finance and war debts. Why had Roosevelt not asked Carter Glass, the venerable senator from Virginia, or Will Woodin, or even the ubiquitous Bernard Baruch? Each had far more expertise and experience than the professor.

Roosevelt obviously was several steps ahead of Moley, who only now was learning about the Allies' war debts. In fact, he was several weeks, perhaps months, ahead of him. He had big plans for Raymond Moley, but he also knew that Moley had absolutely no desire to serve in his administration. He had heard this more than once along the campaign trail. So, the question facing the president-elect was how to bring Moley aboard in an official capacity as of March 4? How could he get the professor to go along with his plans to bring him to Washington?

Defending the New Deal before it even got started was a brilliant ploy. The commitment Moley had shown in staring down Hoover and

Mills was not the stuff of campaign strategy. It was about convictions, and Moley had articulated these convictions in a way that only a true believer might. How else do you take on the two leading experts in the country with four days lead time, and one of them is president of the United States?

Roosevelt's plan was working—better than Raymond Moley could have ever known.

After the Hoover-Mills meeting, Roosevelt finally showed his hand to the professor; it completely blindsided him.

At a Warm Springs meeting with Moley in late November, just days after the fateful war debt meeting, Roosevelt broached the subject of administrative positions. He thought out loud. Louis Howe would be his personal secretary, his "man of mystery." Marvin McIntyre and Stephen Early would handle his official calendar and his press relations. That left open the position of administrative assistant to the president. But Howe would be upset if the position was given to Moley, Roosevelt continued, so he had decided to drop the position altogether.

Moley was stunned. It was all so casual, this conversational buildup to what would be Moley's official position in the administration. Roosevelt had simply assumed away any objections. Rhetorically and interpersonally, it was a risky move. What if it backfired? What if Moley took grave offense at the seemingly cavalier way in which Roosevelt had made the assumption?

Moley did take offense, in a way. He had given up the idea of public office twenty years earlier, he explained to Roosevelt. He wanted to be free to write about and speak about public affairs. He would not wear an official harness that would bind him to "White House cupbearing," "administrative paper-shuffling," and "party goose-stepping."[1] No way. Official office was not for him—not now, not ever.

Roosevelt had figured Moley for just such an answer. "Of course you wouldn't want to be tied down to an administrative job," he agreed. "But that isn't my idea." Roosevelt proceeded to explain that he had found the perfect job for Moley: assistant secretary of state. It was a job "completely free of statutory duty." Roosevelt had indeed been doing his homework. Now came the personal sell.

"Your responsibility would be directly to me. There'd be no en-tanglements either with my secretariat or with any of the Cabinet. Don't you see?" he asked Moley. "You've got to have a job with enough prestige to make it possible for you to deal with people of importance for me. But that's all the title has to mean. Nothing else has to change. We just continue."

Next came the personal hard sell: "I've found it easier to work with you than I have with anyone else. . . . You know my intellectual com-mitments. You know most of the people that we've got to put to work [for a cabinet]. I'd counted on you to keep in touch with the State Department on debts for me, and to get the legislative ball rolling."[2]

This was a remarkable expression of confidence. It was also a remark-able expression of just how hard Roosevelt was leaning on him. All of the important interregnum issues—selecting a cabinet, dealing with the foreign debt issue, and, of course, priming the legislative pump for the New Deal—the president-elect was investing him with tremendous responsibility. Roosevelt had found Moley's soft spot. He had attempted to persuade him with the "only role I could conceivably play in his administration."

Most importantly, Moley did not say no.

The second iteration of the high-stakes Hoover game resumed officially on December 17. Again, the matter involved war debts, but in the span of nearly one month, the complexities had greatly multiplied. With the default by the French on December 15, and with the report of the U.S. representatives to the Preparatory Commission of Experts for the forth-coming World Economic Conference, Herbert Hoover hoped that Roosevelt would finally see the light: namely that war debts could not be divorced from the forthcoming conference, neither could they be divorced from negotiations at the ongoing Conference on World Dis-armament.

On the seventeenth, Roosevelt received another of Hoover's lengthy telegrams. In it, the president expressed his hope that Roosevelt would work with him in selecting a delegation whose task it would be to ne-gotiate war debts as well as to give "coordinate consideration" to the two impending conferences.[3] Hoover clearly had rejected Moley's (and Roosevelt's) idea that normal diplomatic channels be used for negotiating war debts. More importantly, however, Hoover was upping the stakes significantly by linking debts, disarmament, and international economics. The report by his representatives to the Preparatory Commission had seemingly given the president a new and vital card to play in his interregnum bargaining with the president-elect.

Roosevelt telegrammed his reply to Hoover on the evening of December 19. His position was unequivocal: "the questions of disarmament, intergovernmental debts and permanent economic arrangements will be found to require selective treatment." As to the question of Roosevelt cooperating with the president to name a delegation, he was equally clear: "I feel that it would be both improper for me and inadvisable for you, . . . for me to take part in naming representatives." Roosevelt couched his unwillingness to participate in legalistic terms: "it would be unwise for me to accept an apparent joint responsibility with you when, as a matter of constitutional fact, I would be wholly lacking in any attendant authority."[4] In brief, the three pressing matters would simply have to wait until he became president on March 4. If, however, the president wanted to engage in "informal" conferences or "preliminary" economic studies on any of the three matters, why, Roosevelt would not object.

Hoover was not yet done. The day after receiving Roosevelt's telegram, he tried again. He brazenly rejected Roosevelt's position "that cooperation cannot be established between the outgoing and incoming administrations which will give earlier solution and recovery from these difficulties." The issue, as he saw it, was not about war debts or the conferences per se; rather, it was about having the administration machinery in place so that the new administration could put forth its solutions expeditiously once in office. The president closed with the rather forthright suggestion that Roosevelt designate "Mr. Owen D. Young, Colonel House, or any other men of your party possessed of your views and your confidence, and at the same time familiar with these problems, to sit with the principal officers of this administration in endeavor to see what steps can be taken to avoid delays of precious time and inevitable losses that will ensue from such delays."[5]

Roosevelt and Moley read the telegram carefully, and the professor could not help but take this suggestion personally, especially Hoover's statement that the appointee be "familiar with these problems." The president obviously saw him as a nuisance, a gadfly who had no business in such important affairs of state.

Their response was swift and predictable. Roosevelt reiterated in a telegram dispatched on December 21 that the only possible cooperation between the administrations was in the areas of "exploratory work and preliminary surveys." He simply could not commit to any particular policy or policies before March 4. Moreover, for him to appoint someone like a Young or House (Moley was not mentioned) "would suggest the presumption that such representatives were empowered to exchange views on matters of large and binding policy."[6] This was more of a policy commitment than Roosevelt was willing to make. However, as long as Hoover would commit his representatives on either debts or the World Economic Conference to avoid binding the new administration "to any ultimate policy," he would be "happy to receive their information and their expressions of opinion."

Thus, Hoover had, despite the volley of telegrams, lost round two. Or, had he?

Maybe the problem was personal. Maybe Roosevelt simply would not negotiate with him. Perhaps his surrogates were better positioned to get the incoming administration to commit to some of its policies. Maybe. It was worth a try, and Herbert Hoover was getting desperate. He was also running out of time.

Whether Roosevelt, over the course of the next month, did what he did to lure Moley further into the administration or for some other motivation cannot be known. As with so many things, Roosevelt remained a cipher. But the next month would alter forever the way Moley viewed the president-elect. What had seemed so clear in the telegram exchange with Hoover, as well as the earlier meeting with he and Mills was, by Christmas, much less clear. Norman Davis and then Henry

Stimson—to say nothing of Franklin Roosevelt—would greatly complicate the possibility for a domestic New Deal.

Both men had Hoover's blessing to work on the president-elect. If he was truly the problem in the negotiations, there was only one thing left to do: let others act as his surrogates. Moley was completely flummoxed as to why Roosevelt would even agree to meet and negotiate. He thought that the telegram sent on December 21 was the final word on the matter of foreign war debts, disarmament, and international economics. To make matters worse, as Norman Davis sequestered himself with Roosevelt on December 26 and 27, Moley was in Cleveland visiting with family and recovering from an illness.

Davis was a colleague of Roosevelt's from the Wilson administration. He was also a Democrat and the "darling" of the internationalists. As a member of the Organizing Commission of the World Economic Conference and a U.S. delegate to the Disarmament Conference, he was committed to an early resolution of the debt and disarmament issues.

From Cleveland, Moley entrusted Tugwell to be his proxy, especially if Roosevelt's newfound flirtation with the internationalists should get serious. It did, and Tugwell went to Albany on December 26. He found Davis closeted with Roosevelt. A secretary told Tugwell to come back the next morning. Clearly, the governor was listening quite intently to the "other" side. The following morning, Roosevelt explained to Tugwell that he wanted to evaluate Davis's plans alone. He did not give Tugwell the chance to rebut the international position.

To make matters worse, Roosevelt had agreed to Davis's suggestion that he invite Secretary of State Stimson to lunch with him at Hyde Park and talk over the matter of France's apparently new position to make amends for its default—among other international topics. Roosevelt invited Stimson to Hyde Park on January 6. Moley was not even invited to sit in.

The two met on January 9. Their lunch lasted some five hours. Over the course of the next ten days, Moley gradually found out what had transpired. On January 11, 16, and 17, Moley learned in piecemeal fashion that Stimson had secured Roosevelt's agreement on a host of significant foreign policy commitments consistent with the Hoover administration. Roosevelt also "casually" mentioned to the press on the seventeenth that he had agreed to meet with Hoover yet again on the question of war debts.

Moley was "sick at heart" over the agreements. What was happening to all the careful groundwork and planning for a domestic New Deal? How could Roosevelt so cavalierly, and without consultation, approve of such consequential foreign policy measures? Why were war debts back on the bargaining table? Then there was the personal question: Had not Roosevelt given Moley his word at Warm Springs just one month earlier that he would be his chief consultant?

The president-elect was playing his prospective assistant secretary of state like a finely tuned instrument. On the eighteenth, Moley and Tugwell attempted to find out what in the hell was going on with their boss. They did not get very far. However, Moley did finally get an invitation to be back in the policy and planning loop. "Have you any engagements for the 20th?" Roosevelt asked. "I'd like you to go with me to the Hoover meeting."

Moley quickly agreed. Nothing could keep him from attending. Franklin Roosevelt had played his final interregnum card with Raymond Moley.

On the nineteenth, Roosevelt told reporters that Norman Davis would not be accompanying him to the latest Hoover conference. Moley was relieved.

The next day, however, Davis met with Roosevelt and asked the president-elect if he would like to have him accompany him to the conference. Sure, came the reply, he could come along if he wanted.

The two sides again met in the Red Room. This time, in addition to Mills, the president wisely brought with him his ace negotiator, Stimson. Davis, his other negotiator, made it four against one. Who knew where Roosevelt stood at this point.

The question—again—was war debts and economic issues pertaining to the impending World Economic Conference, their combination or separation.

Moley argued as passionately as he could for what he thought he understood to be Roosevelt's position. Roosevelt seemed to revel in all the attention and spirited debate. He eventually sided with the professor: the question of war debts must be separate from other matters. Under the most improbable of circumstances, Raymond Moley had won: the domestic New Deal was still intact. In the course of winning, however, he knew that something far more fundamental and profound had been lost. The ideas, the policy, still mattered, but the trust in those policies and ideas that he thought he shared with Roosevelt had been violated. His initial impressions, the ones he had so thoughtfully penned to Nell back in April, had proven prophetic in the most consequential of ways.

How could he now write an eloquent inaugural address for the man who, up until the eleventh hour, had sold him out? From what inventional resources could he draw, considering his very real disillusionment? He could not have known it at the time, but the inspiration would come—but from a most unsuspecting, and unwanted, source. For now, the professor was "tired and sore at heart."[7] He needed to distract himself, even for a few hours. He decided to attend the opening of Elmer Rice's *We, The People*. He hated it. Afterward, his secretary took him home. He had a bad headache.

Common sense, combined with the events of the past few weeks, told Moley to quit. The stakes were getting too high, and now, at the crucial hour, his boss seemed to have developed a case of weak knees. But it was not on common sense that the professor now leaned. As January turned to February, it was instinct on which the professor now relied—specifically his "Irishman's instinctive squaring off to battle for the thing in which he believes."[8] Franklin Roosevelt had seen to it—twice now—that Moley did battle for "the thing," the core of the New Deal. He had defended the still inchoate program at the highest echelons of power with such passion and conviction that to now leave its future in someone else's hands was simply unconscionable. It was clear that he could not even leave it in Roosevelt's hands. Common sense dictated that he finish quickly and walk away. His instincts and his ego said otherwise.

To make it even less likely that Moley could, or would, simply walk away, Roosevelt had invested him with the not-insignificant responsibility of helping him to recruit a cabinet. So, as Roosevelt was about to begin an eleven-day cruise aboard Vincent Astor's 263-foot motor yacht, the *Nourmahal,* Moley headed to Warm Springs to make plans for the coming month. He also needed to confer with Roosevelt on his own appointment in the administration, and there was still the matter of the inaugural address. Moley had not written a word, and it was now four months since their initial conversation in San Francisco.

On February 2, Moley finally got Roosevelt to commit in writing to what his duties would be as assistant secretary of state. Roosevelt dictated, Moley wrote: "The foreign debts, the World Economic Conference, supervision of the economic advisor's office, and such additional duties as the President may direct in the general field of foreign and domestic government."[9] Moley had to chuckle at this last duty. It was vintage Roosevelt: sufficiently vague, yet certainly broad enough for him to get manifold mileage out of Moley's talents.

With this matter temporarily resolved, Moley finally resumed work on the inaugural address. After dinner on Friday, February 3, as their train chugged south and east toward Jacksonville, Moley sat with Roosevelt in his private car. Joining them was Ed Flynn of New York. This time, Moley took notes; he would not rely on memory for this most important of tasks. On two 6½-by-10½-inch pieces of paper headed "Memorandum," Moley enumerated the first sketch of the ideas that Roosevelt wanted in the speech:

1. Sickness—1 page
    In sickness—strife
2. Failure of us: of all due to method ½ page
3. 10 points—1 page
4. Intra-nat[ional] ½
5. The good neighbor
    Action needed
6. Dictatorship
7. No failure of Dem[ocracy]
8. Tribute to people of U.S.
    encourage them[10]

After listing the eight points, Moley figured that he had better sketch the ideas just a bit more fully. On a second piece of paper, he wrote:

> Sick world—
>> Forged into unity by rings of fire
> A part of this is because *we*
>> are sick
> The failure of method not of
>> substance
> The failure of incentives
> The failure of balance
>> intra
> No past to ignore—this put
>> into
> good neighbor
> To meet w.[ith] dictatorial powers[11]

Some of the themes Moley immediately recognized from the campaign. The theme of sickness, for example, had been a staple—both from the back platform of the Roosevelt Special as well as in his carefully prepared remarks. The irony had not escaped Moley: Here was a recovering paralytic, a man many perceived to be terribly sick himself, who was figuring the nation as prostrate from illness. Of course, the figuration was not original with Roosevelt; Moley had been reading about the nation's "poor health" for nearly three years. As a practicing rhetorician, it made sense to him: How else but through the body would economic suffering be internalized and understood? Hoover, however, had made the sickness largely a mental matter—a lack of confidence, a patient's unwillingness to believe that recovery was imminent.

Did Roosevelt really mean to emphasize that this sickness had spread to the entire world? Had not their repeated interactions with Stimson, Davis, Hoover, and Mills all pointed toward domestic recovery as the first priority? A sick world would have to wait for its sick leader to heal first. Or, figured differently, a "good neighbor" should not act abroad before first acting at home. "Action" was "needed," but not immediate action abroad. Moley and Roosevelt had seen all hope of an interregnum New Deal go up in smoke by February 1. The farm bill, farm-mortgage relief, bankruptcy legislation, repeal of the Eighteenth Amendment, tax plans, and government finance—all looked bleak by January's close. Roosevelt would have to call a special session of Congress immediately, so his inaugural address would have to serve as a sort of legislative harbinger. Intranationalism would take first priority. Ceremonial speechmaking was a luxury, one that on March 4 the new administration could not afford.

In addition, any thought of an inaugural address rooted in generic staples was dispatched in point number six: "dictatorship." Of all the rhetorical familiarities of an American presidential inaugural address, this was a term most foreign to it. A president simply did not invoke this term—unless, perhaps, he was disparaging or characterizing a form of government or leadership wholly separate from democracy. Yet, point number six on Moley's list did not refer to another country or a menace from abroad. No, the term was being employed intranationally, as an opening salvo for the administration. Desperation had long ago passed; to even utter the word "dictatorship" in the context of American governance was to potentially profane the nation's most important legacy. However, on February 3, just a month before taking office, Franklin Roosevelt not only bandied the term about, it was also—for the moment at least—an important part of this most important of speeches.

And there—right below the dread d-word, democracy's anathema—was the reassuring phrase "no failure of Dem." How could "dictatorship" square with such a sentiment? It was almost as if Roosevelt, Moley, and Flynn had quickly responded to number six with number seven. Number eight could not offer such reassurance. No, seven had to go with six—if six was going to be uttered at all. Moley and his interlocutors went further by qualifying this dread term. Better to have it as an adjective than a noun: "dictatorial powers" did not necessarily make Franklin Roosevelt a dictator in the way that "dictatorship" clearly did. But what were the men talking about, what would coax the president into a "meet"-ing? With who or what would he be meeting? Something or someone was clearly pushing him to react in such an aggressive manner. Would the American people stand for such a bold confrontation on the very first day of his administration? Was a threat already in order? Some honeymoon period.

In actuality, what looked like a grave threat to be invoked by the new president on inauguration day was not quite so grave. Nor was it novel. Just the day before, on February 2 on the Senate floor, "dictatorship" got what would be the first of several favorable public hearings. Roosevelt had paved the way for that initial hearing at a meeting in late December with several congressional Democrats. During the campaign, most notably in a speech in Pittsburgh, Roosevelt had pledged his administration to drastic economies: a 25 percent across-the-board cut in the federal government's operating expenses. To affect such economies, Roosevelt informed his congressional colleagues that he wanted (and needed) broad powers of executive reorganization and authorization. If the lame-duck Seventy-second Congress could give him anything, it might be able to deliver on this since it would relieve them of the need to make unpopular fiscal choices. He also knew that Hoover would likely sign a bill giving the president broad powers of reorganization given his December 9 plan to regroup fifty-eight federal agencies.

The matter was formally introduced in an amendment to the Treasury–Post Office Bill, H.R. 13520. Title IV of the amendment would occupy Congress for much of February. More specifically, just how much authority Congress was willing to cede to Roosevelt would engender rancorous debate in both houses. What was perhaps less contentious, ironically, was the name: All seemed to agree that sweeping powers of reorganization might rightly be called dictatorial.

On February 2, the discourse of dictatorship was officially written into the Senate record. To his colleagues, Sen. R. S. Copeland (D–New York) noted, "I understand by Title IV we are conferring extraordinary powers upon the President—practically dictatorial powers."[12] As he saw it, the purpose of the reorganization part of the bill "is to give to the President the power to do anything that he may see fit to do in the reorganization of the departments." But there was good reason for such vast authority: "We are proposing to give him power such as no President ever had, in my opinion, even in war time. However, we have an emergency which demands it; I recognize that."

Less than twenty-four hours later, Moley, Roosevelt, and Flynn had strategically appropriated the discourse of dictatorship for the inaugural address. It was, after all, not an arrogant play for power but simply a legislative extension of executive authority.

As for the other points Moley had enumerated, numbers one and two just did not seem to go together. Number two was mechanistic: a sickness usually was not a failure. Certainly, sickness, according to germ theory, was no longer considered a moral failure. Sickness, as Roosevelt knew only too well, was frighteningly random. Still, maybe the conversation was not metaphorical. After all, Moley had elaborated, "a part of this is because *we* are sick." A part of what? How could a "sick world" exist, yet only a "part" of it be due to sickness? Then again, maybe the nation was not sick. Sickness, physical sickness, typically involved one's "substance," and yet the "failure" was of method, not substance—and it involved "all" of us.

Moreover, what "method" had failed? It clearly had not been a failure of democracy, dictatorship notwithstanding. Was it a method of commerce that had failed? A method of leadership? Maybe it was a failure of the method used to diagnose sickness in the nation's collective faith. Maybe Hoover had been right all along: maybe the sickness *was* one of pessimism.

Yet, method was not the only failure. There were also the twin failures of incentives and balance. The idea of balance had been a favorite of Roosevelt's for as long as Moley had worked with him. Specifically, Roosevelt believed that the nation had for too long ignored the plight of the American farmer, and that as long as the farmer was broke, the nation's purchasing power would be seriously out of kilter or "balance." Furthermore, the nation needed to rebalance its population. Too many people had given up on the family farm and migrated to the city. This needed to be changed in order to achieve balance. In many respects, this was a zero-sum game: A loss for farmers was a gain for urban dwellers, and a loss for the cities was a gain for farmers. This was a closed economic model. It was also an interdependent one in which agrarians and urbanites needed each other, whether they knew it or not. In such a zero-sum economic game, perhaps the day of "enlightened administration" that Roosevelt had so famously stated at the Commonwealth Club had indeed arrived. The economic frontier perhaps had closed, and it was left to the experts now to divvy up—rebalance—the gains and losses. Yet, how could such a view be squared with America's economic past? If the past was not to be ignored, what then of America's frontier days? Had not industrialization brought the nation great wealth? Just what had Roosevelt taken away from Frederick Jackson Turner's seminar at Harvard?

Finally, what incentives had failed? Had the profit motive itself imploded on a steady diet of stock speculation fed by greedy margin buying? Had the incentive to get ahead financially through rapidly realized paper profits replaced the incentive to work for one's wages? Then again, if the selfish profit motive was alive and well, why were businesses not securing loans at low rates of interest and why were the stock speculators not purchasing heavily discounted stocks? If wages were low, why were companies not hiring? Finally, if farmers were overproducing, why were so many people not eating?

The freewheeling discussion continued into the night as the train plodded along toward north Florida's east coast. Moley recorded no thoughts mingling religion and the inaugural address.

Roosevelt was very much looking forward to escaping from the daily din that now accompanied his every waking moment. Save for occasional telegram contact, he would be blissfully ignorant of events on terra firma. He anticipated the fishing, the swimming, and, of course, the drinking, card playing, and general tomfoolery with the fellows. He certainly loved the sea.

Moley had other plans—namely, writing a speech and recruiting a cabinet. But before heading back to New York and Washington, the professor was scheduled to get a little rest and recreation as Joseph Kennedy's guest at his Palm Beach estate. However, Moley could not give himself over to mindless cogitations of sun and surf. He still had a speech to write, and he wanted to get a few more thoughts down before the rush of time and other events obscured Friday night's conversation. Before he could actually write the speech, though, he needed more ideas, more metaphors, more striking allusions—something upon which to hang the inaugural message. Sickness simply could not be the master metaphor of this speech, especially with the urgent and emphatic note of "*action needed.*" A sick people could not be expected to participate in bold, decisive action. Yet, as Moley remembered from their September conversation, he could not just pretend that suffering did not exist and that optimism was in the air. People were suffering, had been suffering, and would likely suffer much more before the president-elect's New Deal could cure the body politic. Some sort of inspiration was needed, especially if the nation was going to be acting together after March 4.

Moley pulled out his legal pad and tried out a few ideas. "The state of the union." No, how about, "The dark state of the union?" Sandwiched between these sentiments was an underlined phrase, "The discredited captains." He had heard the "captains of industry" expression before, and since he did not want to blame the people for their depressed economic plight, why not target the top? It was in keeping with his Forgotten Man speech, in which Roosevelt had railed against those at "the top of the social and economic structure." Roosevelt also wanted to avoid igniting class warfare on March 4, an accusation that had been leveled against him by Al Smith in the immediate aftermath of that speech on April 7.

So, Moley returned to a phrase that he had jotted down on February 3: "Forged into unity by rings of fire." Unity had been a common motif during the campaign, but this was a near-verbatim, poaching from Wilson's 1917 inaugural address. Moley moved to modify it: "We in the U.S. are forged into a new unity with the fire that burns throughout the world." But the allusion was a bit too hellish and a bit too internationalist, so he moved to temper it: "The larger hopes center upon this one— the symbol of unity." What that "symbol" would be remained uncertain, but there would be no place for the rugged individualist by March 4. In fact, Moley consulted Emerson on the matter; he noted that on page ninety-three, Emerson inveighed against "Everything that tends to insulate the individual." He expanded the thought: "because to live by ourselves is not to." If Roosevelt hoped to achieve unity of purpose and action, he would have to convince the American people that economic individualism would only exacerbate their problems. There simply would have to be some sacrifice, a collective "discipline"—the word Moley had stumbled upon with Roosevelt back at the Palace Hotel. The time had come when the nation "cannot exist on [the] private profit motive."[13]

Moley turned his thoughts to Roosevelt. Beyond the high-minded ideas and finely wrought metaphors, the president-elect was a man in whom people needed to believe. Moley knew that the people's profound disaffection for the publicly taciturn and diffident Hoover could be readily transformed into an admiration and even affection for their new, publicly ebullient president. He personally knew Roosevelt to be a tremendously likable, charming man. The nation should know this, too. Moley scribbled, "Faith, reassurance—stay with me." Was the faith in question a personal faith in Roosevelt's political program? Was it a more profound faith, a civic faith in the goodness of America's fundamental mission? Moley seemed to answer that it was the latter: "M[ose]'s 40 days in the desert." It was the first overtly religious reference for the inaugural address, and it was a most suggestive parallel. Why Moses' forty days and not Christ's? What sort of commandments would Roosevelt proffer? Would they have the status of economic orthodoxy? What sorts of false idols had the people been worshiping? Beyond the thematic issues were the formal. The hierarchical patterns were unmistakable: Would Roosevelt descend to the masses after careful consultation with the economic elite? Maybe Moses was not such a good parallel after all.

Beyond the religious, beyond the metaphorical and the economic, was style. Whatever came from Roosevelt's lips on March 4, it should be memorable, striking, even aphoristic. Moley experimented with antithesis and parallelism: "The world was made for man—not man for the world." That was too general. He tried again: "not be ministered unto but to minister." There, again, another overtly religious reference. The religious, it seemed, was slowly winning out over the mechanistic.

Moley figured it was again time to try for some orderly expression. This would be his third outline. He scratched a Roman numeral I on the left margin of his legal pad, and listed several subpoints under the heading, "Sick nation in midst of sick world":

Stoppage of business
Frozen exchange
Withered enterprises-institutions
broken—bankrupt

Next to this cluster of four points, Moley wrote in the left margin, "The Withered leaves of industrial enterprise lie on every side." He then continued listing subpoints:

Befuddled leaders
People
Where there is no vision the people perish
We
In the heavy air of

While the thoughts were far from complete, the early metaphorical patterns suggested an earthly naturalism of dying and death. The "withered leaves" bespoke an industrial autumn, in much the same way that a "frozen exchange" alluded to a winter tariff. Similarly, Moley's reference to "the heavy air" suggested thickness, immobility—a difficulty in drawing air. He had indeed painted, albeit in crude stick figures, a picture of a sick nation, perhaps a nation no longer even convalescing, but one on the brink of death. Of course, the naturalism in question was cyclical and therefore predictable: fall and winter would in due time yield to the rebirth seasons of spring and summer. It was a most secular thought.

On the bottom half of the page were the points comprising Roman numeral II:

This failure is due to method—not
substance—no shortage—not failure
of nature—not even human
nature—but of mechanics and method—
leadership—the traditional modes of
relief have—the philosophy of

money changers has failed—
overproduction
End
Not to be ministered unto but
to minister
Not to save banks
Restore values—(equities)[14]

Very early in the drafting process, the three themes of naturalism, mechanization and method, and religion battled it out in Moley's imagination. There was nothing wrong with nature, inclusive of human nature. However, if the sole cause of the nation's economic problems was in "mechanics and method," why invoke an entire "philosophy?" And if this philosophy was capitalism itself, what of the insidious and unmistakable reference to the "money changers?" If Christ expelled the money changers from the temple, was Roosevelt the new Messiah of a revised moral capitalism? In the left margin, Moley wrote, "As the money changers were driven from the temple—so it behooves us to restore moral values by driving out—material standards." Roosevelt was no Christ; it would be up to the citizens, in Moley's formulation, to become Christlike. The nation's collective "ministry" was nothing short of a transformed economic order.

Maybe Raymond Moley was just playing with possibilities. Maybe he was badly confused. As he returned to New York from his working vacation, the inaugural address clearly needed more of his attention. Yes, his concentrated attention. Moley pulled out his pocket calendar and blocked off Sunday the twelfth and Monday the thirteenth as days on which he would do concentrated work on the speech. On Sunday, he worked in isolation at his small office at Barnard College. Late in the evening, at 11:30, Moley wrote at the top of his legal pad, "Final." This would be his final outline before writing a first draft of the speech. The outline combined work that he had done in both north and south Florida. The master organizing term was still sickness.

Final   11:30 P.M.
  Sunday
Sick Nations
  The Failure
  Cause of Failure
  Bad Leaders
  Money changers
  The Phil[osophy] in people
  Wholesome values lost sight of
  This a moral failure too
    honest politics and business
Rehabilitation—10 points or so
  Our house in order
The Good Neighbor
How to get it
Disciplined action—purgation
  —repeal—hypocrisy—
Under dictatorship if necessary
No essential failure of Democ[racy]
Tribute to people[15]

The outline for the inaugural address was shaping up to consist of a standard problem/solution approach. Moley had also made some important changes. He knew that Roosevelt had to walk a fine line between blaming the people for selfishly seeking profits and praising them for their patience and courage. Thus, it was the philosophy that was *in* and not the philosophy *of* the people. The latter was more permanent, agreed upon—an outward manifestation of an internal state. The former was more artificial; something created and constructed. Like a bacterium that had invaded the body, a philosophy of greed had temporarily infected the body politic. Wholesome values would surely return if only they were seen in a positive light.

But the American people were not being—and should not be—blamed for the greatest measure of the failure. Roosevelt had frequently emphasized during the campaign that he had no problem with

Republicans; in fact, he courted them. The Republican leaders had raised his ire. Even more specifically, if it was not Hoover's lack of public leadership on economic affairs, it was his incorrigible tendency to see the problem merely in rhetorical terms: If only the people would believe, much, materially, would improve. As far as Hoover was concerned, no tribute to the people was possible; they were to blame for much of the mess over which he had presided.

Moley remembered that Roosevelt had not given a speech on foreign policy during the campaign. He did not want to muddy the campaign waters any further by detracting from his domestic plans. He also did not want to invoke an expert's wrath on a subject he was not then well equipped to handle. On March 4, Roosevelt would continue this strategy, one that Moley had fought for with all his mind and soul. The United States would be a "good neighbor" in foreign affairs, but beyond that, the nation first needed to get its own "house in order." The metaphors were quaint, simple. At a time when domesticity was threatened by uncertainty, unemployment, and the specter of hunger, it was only natural for Roosevelt to return to that idealized image of the home. The other "neighbors" could, and would, certainly wait.

The sickness, while it required "purgation" and "rehabilitation," continued to run afoul of the need for action. From their first conversation on the inaugural address, both Moley and Roosevelt understood that the country would demand action by March 4. But how could a sick people participate in such action? Sickness and action, particularly "disciplined action," simply did not go together. Moley, however, liked the new formulation. He had suggested the word "discipline" for the speech back in September. On February 12, it finally returned, and the term lost some of its harshness when paired with "action."

There was also, again, the other problematic pairing of dictatorship and democracy. Moley did not yet want to give up on the seemingly contradictory sentiments, so he continued to tinker. He added an important qualifier: There had been no "essential" failure of democracy. Moreover, if democracy in its essence had not failed, and it did not appear headed to failure in the future, perhaps the draconian term could be smuggled in—but only as a threat to a recalcitrant Congress. If the term was going to remain in the speech, it simply had to be followed or preceded by democratic reassurances. Moley perhaps knew he was being a bit cautious with the term dictatorship. But the gravity of the term, especially invoked in an inaugural address, required the handling of the gem cutter. He was well aware of the so-called dictatorship debate, especially the one that was raging in the House over the reorganization amendment. As far as the House minority leader, Rep. B. H. Snell (R–New York), was concerned, Roosevelt would simply have too much power: "I shall oppose giving any executive carte blanche authority to re-organize and abolish the entire executive department of government. Those provisions would make an absolute dictator of Mr. Roosevelt. It would give him more power than any executive in the world except Mussolini."[16] Americans, Snell concluded, were "not ready for a Mussolini . . . if we are we better abolish Congress and go home." His Republican colleague, Representative Chindbloom of Illinois, was more sanguine: "I am in favor of giving the President every power we can bestow, and to those afraid we may go too far, I want to suggest that this may be more acceptable than it appears."[17] At this point in the debate, neither Moley nor Roosevelt knew whether they would get an executive reorganization bill or not. Even so, with or without the legislation, their Progressive ally from California, Hiram Johnson, wrote ominously to his sons, "We are, . . . much closer to a sort of dictatorship in this country than we have been during our lives."[18] For the time being, dictatorship could remain as a topical point in the address.

Moley shook his head and looked at his outline. He liked the metaphor of the money changers. Like any good metaphor, it did a lot of work. In this case, it indicted with Messianic certainty an entire class. By the same token, it was sufficiently vague to allow even the most unscrupulous money changers to avoid the public scorn of being singled out—be they Democrat or Republican.

Finally, before calling it a night, Moley added his first marginal note on delivery and tone. In the left margin, next to the reference to a "moral failure," he wrote, "giving them hell." Moley envisioned Roosevelt thundering away at the bully pulpit, letting loose in a manner perhaps reminiscent of the cousin who had preceded him to the White House. Moley had seen Roosevelt play the righteously indignant role. The question nevertheless remained: Was the inaugural address the appropriate setting for invective, even vague invective?

The following day, Moley attempted to move beyond the outline form. He needed to move beyond ideational invention to prosaic composition because the speech was only nineteen days away. It was always the hardest part of the process. Today, Monday, February 13, was no different—save for the fact that the writing came even more laboriously than usual. Even so, he kept his two assistants, Celeste Jedel (who was taking dictation for Moley's diary) and Annette Pomeranz, nearby to transfer his handwritten notes into a typescript manuscript.

Part I of the inaugural began: "America is a sick nation in the midst of a sick world. We are sick because of our failure to recognize economic changes in time, and to make provision against their consequences."[19] This sounded like some sort of Hooverian disquisition on structural economics—with a metaphor thrown in for good rhetorical measure. Things only got worse from this dismal opening. Moley elaborated that, more than other factors, "the machine age" was to blame for altering the structural relations among man, machine, and productive capacity. The other "factor" contributing to the sickness was that trade had "frozen." No elaboration, just a one-sentence causal claim.

Then the pessimism kicked in: "It is time to face the facts and get away from the idea that we can return to conditions that approximate those of four years ago." Prosperity, it seemed, was a "condition" that could not hope to be attained. But even to try "to attempt to rebuild precisely what we had before is to invite the pain and suffering that we incurred in its failure." The whole diseased organism of capitalism, come to think of it, needed to be rethought: "it is necessary, moreover, to bend the entire theory of human progress away from the strivings for private money making, so characteristic of the past." Nothing in Ray Moley's outline contained such anticapitalistic sentiments. They suggested that the problem was not in the system, but with people who had abused it.

Instead of the old order of capitalism, the country needed an "evolution into [the] new." That evolution would not be brought about by the traditional means of natural selection. Instead, it "must be guided by informed and enlightened thought, with no disposition to reject experimental and tentative efforts merely because they are new and untried." Moley was relying on campaign platitudes, ones that had "worked" at Oglethorpe University and the Commonwealth Club. But this was no campaign, and if Roosevelt was calling for the end of profit-driven capitalism, Moley had damn well better come up with something with a bit more bite than experimentation and enlightened bureaucracy.

Part I stunk. If it did not read like an academic treatise all the way through, then it read like a primer on socialism with a Darwinian bent. Moley decided to try some other issue. He turned to the "Good Neighbor." Clearly, having been through a crash course on international economics, war debts, and foreign policy generally, he could do better than Part I.

"The good neighbor," he wrote, "knows when to mind his own business." This was good homespun wisdom—not quite inaugural caliber, maybe, but not bad. Then came some decidedly nonhomespun neighborly talk: "He is not moved or deceived by the unsubstantial and sometimes trivial results of broad pretensions of interrelationships." Broad pretensions of interrelationships? Even Herbert Hoover at his rhetorical worst could do better than that. Even Henry Stimson at his arcane diplomatic best could not have topped this one. Moley seemed to be driving at the question of war debts. Maybe.

This was confirmed in the next paragraph: "Basic in the relationship of neighbors is respect for the principle that what is lent should be returned. . . . The relations of a world of neighbors are disturbed profoundly when the distinction is lost between a loan and a gift." The implication was clear: France and England had best continue to pay their war debts. But what was this heavy-handed diplomatic lesson doing in the inaugural address? Had Moley not argued vociferously in both meetings with Hoover that each debtor country should get a hearing with the United States regarding its debt? Even more importantly, if the New Deal was going to be fundamentally premised on domestic reforms, why dwell upon "bad neighbors?" This part was almost as bad as Part I. It was clear to Moley that he was sorely lacking inspiration. Perhaps he missed the hurly-burly of the campaign when he had to write quality speeches—often at a moment's notice. Yet now, with only one speech to write and time on his hands, Moley grappled awkwardly with this, his most important assignment of all.

Perhaps Louis Howe somehow sensed that Moley needed to get away from the daily grind of trying to recruit a cabinet and to draft an inaugural address. Perhaps he needed some respite from all the heavy Washington talk of dictatorship and the end of capitalism. Or, perhaps Howe just wanted Moley in Miami to inform Roosevelt firsthand about the goings-on of the past, eventful eleven days. Whatever the case, Moley had Howe to thank for being in Miami on February 15. The events of that evening, coupled with what happened two days later, seemed somehow to elevate the speech to a loftier, more eloquent perspective. God knows that by mid-February, Raymond Moley needed some perspective, but he surely had not bargained for quite this much.

CHAPTER SIX

February 15–17, 1933

Truth be told, Ray Moley really did not want to travel all the way to Miami just to give Roosevelt the most recent updates, particularly on matters related to recruiting a cabinet. Could not the matter simply wait until the seventeenth or eighteenth, when Roosevelt would be back in New York? Why not a telegram or a phone call? Moley and Louis Howe had actually gotten quite inventive when it came to sending the president-elect important, surreptitious messages while he was at sea. In their search for a treasury secretary, for example, Howe and Moley had reported to Roosevelt: "Prefer a wooden roof to a glass roof over swimming pool. Luhowray."[1] It took Roosevelt some time to decipher the code, but he finally got it: Howe and Moley would prefer William Woodin to Virginia senator Carter Glass.

On top of the lengthy trip was the additional matter of a speech that Moley was scheduled to deliver on Friday, February 17, in Cincinnati. Moreover, he had also been invited to attend a dean's party at Columbia that same day. Louis, though, would not relent: Not only did he want Moley to break the latest cabinet news to Roosevelt in the flesh, but he did not trust Jim Cox and Mitchell Palmer, two men who would likely be around the president-elect in Miami. Louis hated both of them. He also told the professor that "somebody must keep the Gov[ernor] from being too friendly [i.e., agreeable]."[2] He insisted it was the professor's patriotic duty to go.

Perhaps with visions of the Stimson-Davis-Hoover near-debacle in his mind, Moley finally, but reluctantly, agreed to Howe's entreaties. Fortunately, Trubee Davison, an old friend serving as the assistant secretary of war in charge of air operations, had agreed to help salvage his speaking and party engagements: Davison would have an army plane pick up the professor at Jacksonville, on the sixteenth, for a flight north to New York and then southern Ohio. He also might be able to help Moley fly south as well.

The professor departed at 2:30 in the afternoon on Tuesday, February 14. He resignedly took the train. The weather had been too poor for him to enlist Davison's services for a plane ride down. The next day, after arriving in Jacksonville, Moley got a flight to Miami where he would meet up with the president-elect that evening.

The massive *Nourmahal* reached port at Pier One of Miami's municipal docks at 7 P.M. on the fifteenth. Reporters soon pressed in around the effervescent and tanned president-elect. He had had a grand time: "I didn't even open the briefcase. . . . We fished and swam. . . . We went to a different place each day. Usually we fished in the morning and came back to the yacht for lunch."[3] He also informed the small gathering of reporters that he had already locked up the yacht's log so that they could not report on the mischief and hijinks that had taken place on the cruise. Moley noted that Roosevelt was in gay spirits, buoyant and happy, vibrant and alive.

On the campaign trail, Eleanor Roosevelt had often appeared nervous before large crowds of assembled listeners who had gathered to hear her husband's extemporaneous remarks. She wondered if there was someone in the throng who meant to do her husband bodily harm. With only the local police providing security, and often patchwork security at best, the threats seemed palpable. Her immobile husband seemed unconcerned. In response to a congressman's warning on the subject, Roosevelt had responded, "I remember T. R. [Theodore Roosevelt] saying to me, 'The only real danger from an assassin is from one who does not care whether he loses his own life in the act or not. Most of the crazy ones can be spotted first.'"[4] But he had not quite completed the thought, for his famous cousin had also been struck by a would-be-assassin's gunfire during a 1912 campaign swing through Milwaukee. Moreover, had not T. R. ascended to the Oval Office by dint of his boss' assassination?

Ray Moley had been a young boy at the time of William McKinley's assassination—fifteen to be exact. Moley knew exactly how old he was at the time of the killing for a very good reason: he had been there. While he had not actually witnessed the shooting at the Temple of Music at the Buffalo Pan-American Exposition on September 6, 1901, the young Moley was in a small crowd when the mentally ill anarchist, Leon Czolgosz, was brought out on his way to a local prison. The impressionable boy had also seen the frenzied crowd attempt to tear the assassin away from the police.

The president-elect was scheduled to give a brief talk to a large assemblage of well-wishers at nearby Bay Front Park. Three cars set out for the park shortly after 9 P.M. In the lead car, a green touring Buick with the top down, was Roosevelt, Press Secretary Marvin McIntyre, bodyguard Gus Gennerich, Miami mayor Redmond Gautier, and Secret Service agent Robert Clark. Fitzhugh Lee, a Miami policeman, was the driver. Immediately behind the president-elect's car was a convertible carrying Secret Service agents. The third and final car in the caravan, a small sedan, carried Vincent Astor, William Rhinelander Stewart, Kermit Roosevelt, and Moley. Stewart, Astor, and Moley shared the cramped backseat. As they passed along a long row of darkened palms that fronted the ocean along Biscayne Boulevard, Astor raised the specter of assassination. He gestured toward the crowds along the streets and noted, "Anyone could shoot him in such a place as this."[5] Moley responded somewhat offhandedly that this sort of scene was *de rigeur* on the campaign trail. He had seen Roosevelt in large crowds many times, including the one lining Market Street in San Francisco, where eager onlookers had mobbed the president-elect's car. The scene in Miami was no big deal. After all, the Secret Service had joined the security detail, unlike the ragtag operations characteristic of the campaign trail.

As the cars pulled up in front of the amphitheater, the massive gathering, estimated later at twenty-five thousand, must have surprised Moley. The park was so packed with people that Roosevelt's car seemed to be enveloped by them. Most people were standing. Roosevelt was lifted up so that he was sitting on the top of the car's backseat. Someone handed him a loudspeaker, and he began cheerily:

> Mr. Mayor, my friends of Miami: I am not a stranger here because for a good many years I used to come down here. I have not been here for seven years, but I am coming back, for I have firmly resolved not to make this the last time.
>
> I have had a very wonderful twelve days' fishing in these Florida and Bahama waters. It has been a splendid rest and we have caught a great many fish, but I am not going to attempt to tell you any fishing stories. The only fly in the ointment on my trip has been that I have put on about ten pounds so that means that among the other duties that I shall have to perform when I get North is taking those ten pounds off.
>
> I hope very much to be able to come down here next winter, and to see all of you, and to have another enjoyable ten days or two weeks in Florida waters.
>
> Many thanks.[6]

Roosevelt slid down into the car's backseat as the dignitaries on the platform moved quickly down to talk with him. Most notable among them was Chicago's mayor, Anton Cermak. "Tony," as Roosevelt called him, had hoped to meet with the president-elect in Warm Springs in early February, but the plans had fallen through, so here he was, a long way from home, hoping to make amends with the soon-to-be president. Cermak had committed a tactical error back in June, when his city hosted the Democratic National Convention. The mayor had cast his lot with Al Smith because he and the entire Illinois delegation opposed Roosevelt's candidacy. To make matters worse, Smith had been a sore loser, not even waiting for Roosevelt to arrive before leaving town. Cermak hoped to at least get a brief hearing tonight. Not many cities had been hit by the depression as hard as Chicago, and Cermak had ideas about possible federal assistance in the form of loans from the Reconstruction Finance Corporation.

Cermak chatted briefly with Roosevelt from beside the car. Then, as he walked toward the rear of the car, at 9:35, five loud shots rang out. It was gunfire—and it came from nearby. Cermak was hit in the lower right abdomen. He dropped to his knees, but was soon lifted to his feet by L. L. Lee, Miami's city manager, and W. W. Wood, a county committeeman. He appeared to be going rapidly into shock.

The chief Secret Service agent, George Broadnax, yelled to Roosevelt's driver, Fitzhugh Lee, "Get him the hell out of here!"[7] Roosevelt called for him to stop. Broadnax again yelled for Lee to move. Again, Roosevelt told him to stop. He wanted Cermak lifted into his car because it would be the first to reach the hospital. After Lee and Wood hoisted the mayor inside, Roosevelt swung his meaty left arm around Cermak and checked for a pulse. He could not find one. As the car moved out of the park, Miami's chief detective sat on the left-rear mudguard. "I don't think he is going to last," he said. The intended victim of the assassination replied reluctantly, "I am afraid he isn't."[8]

Shortly after they made that grim prognosis, Cermak straightened up from his hunched position in the backseat. Roosevelt finally felt his pulse. He began talking to the mayor, doing his best to reassure the fallen Cermak: "Tony, keep quiet—don't move. It won't hurt you if you keep quiet."

Back at the park, the police had apprehended the shooter: a five-foot-one-inch, thirty-three-year-old unemployed bricklayer named Giuseppe "Joseph" Zangara. To get him out of the mob and harm's way, the police decided to transport him in the car carrying Astor, Stewart, Roosevelt, and Moley. The police put Zangara horizontally across the car's trunk rack and two police officers pinned him there throughout the ride to Jackson Memorial Hospital. Ray Moley assisted by holding onto one of the police officers' belt.

At the hospital, Moley was relieved to see that Roosevelt had not been hurt. In fact, as their car approached the entrance, Roosevelt was walking through the door, leaning on the steady arm of his personal bodyguard, Gennerich. The party decided to remain at the hospital to get periodic reports on Cermak's condition. At about midnight, Moley and Frederic Kernochan, a New York City judge and guest on the

Nourmahal, decided to interrogate the suspect. Clearly, the man had intended to murder the future president. Moley specifically wanted to determine if the motive was explicitly political; he was hoping that it was not.

The two men found a disturbed prisoner on the twenty-first floor of the Dade County Jail. The little man complained about physical pain near his stomach. He said that he wanted to shoot "big men." Beyond this, Moley and Kernochan could determine no overtly political motive. Zangara did, however, possess an important link to Moley's past: The shooter had been carrying a news clipping about McKinley's assassination in his pocket.

The professor emerged from the meeting wanting to get a quick and decisive message to the press: This was no politically motivated assassination attempt but rather the act of a physically sick man who wanted to take out his frustrations on an influential person. Moley laid bare his own motives a few days later to a friend: "I interviewed Zangara after the shooting that night and in my opinion no psychiatrist would declare him insane in the legal sense of the word. I made it very clear in my statement to the newspapers after examining him that I found no political ideas. I did this not only because it was true, but because I felt it was desirable to avoid, so far as possible, any hysteria on the subject of radicalism."[9] The last thing Moley wanted to communicate to the nation was that there were other Zangaras out there, spurred on to kill by the tottering edifice of capitalism. Zangara needed to be seen as an isolated kook, unaffiliated with a network of fellow radicals. If the country could only wait two and a half more weeks, the domestic New Deal could begin to take shape. This was no time for desperation to take hold.

The press took Moley's cue. Zangara's actions were not really about politics, they were instead about the would-be assassin's southern European ethnicity: "Most illiterate dagoes have the killer instinct," *Time* reported, trying to be reassuring, "especially when their animal comfort is disturbed."[10] That many Italians might have been "uncomfortable" at the height of the Great Depression seemed lost upon the writers. But then again, what mattered were looks and appearances—the visible—not the sinister and invisible world of political ideas. Zangara's looks explained the action and vice versa. As with all forms of racism, it was most reassuring.

Instead of boarding the train that evening, which had been the original plan, Roosevelt decided to spend the night aboard the *Nourmahal*. The picture began to emerge: the president-elect had been terribly fortunate on at least two accounts. First, the large crowd combined with Zangara's short stature conspired to make Roosevelt a difficult target to hit—despite being less than ten yards away. Second, the wobbly park chair on which Zangara was standing, plus the quick thinking and bravery of a nearby spectator, Mrs. Lillian Cross, had thrown the man off balance. The fact of Roosevelt's good fortune in the face of lethal threat suggested to Moley that the president-elect might be on emotional tenterhooks in the early morning hours in the safe confines of the docked yacht. And who would not be? To have someone empty a revolver at you just a few yards from where you were sitting would give even the most hardened veteran pause.

Not Roosevelt.

Aboard the *Nourmahal* that night, Moley looked for any and every indication that might suggest that Roosevelt had emerged from Bay Front Park physically unscathed but emotionally wounded. In his powers of observation—and they were acute—he saw nothing. The attempt on the president-elect's life had not seemed to faze him in the least. What Ray Moley did not know then, perhaps could not have known, was the extent to which the "Roosevelt way" of dealing with emotional or physical trauma was to keep a "stiff upper lip."

Franklin Roosevelt allowed many people into his company. Since the summer of 1921, most people had to come to him because of his immobility. But any emotional connection was reserved for only his closest companions—and even they seemed only to get occasional glimpses, never a steady, trusting disclosure. Perhaps Roosevelt was genuinely terrified and shaken that night as he rested aboard the *Nourmahal*. Perhaps not. But if the president-elect could stare down a would-be assassin, if he could selflessly comfort and care for a fallen man in the midst of chaos and mortal danger, then perhaps the nation had picked the right man back in November. The depression, after all, was fundamentally of a material nature. As such, perhaps it posed no grave threat. The country could and would endure.

Maybe sickness was the wrong master metaphor for the inaugural address. After the events of February 15, there were no more allusions to it in Moley's drafts. Maybe Louis Howe was privy to the ineffable and the uncanny in ways that a professor never would be. Whatever it was, Moley was grateful to have been with Roosevelt on that fateful night. If nothing else, Moley could offer the nation his reassurance that revolution was not in the offing. He had also borne witness to a tremendous act of bravery. The courtship with Stimson, Davis, and the internationalists, and the nonchalant manner of his own courting in the administration were really quite trivial matters. He could perhaps see for the first time. For the lucky ones, after death or the threat of death comes perspective. In any event, Ray Moley got more of it than he perhaps needed—certainly much more than he wanted.

He still had his speaking engagement in Cincinnati to attend on the seventeenth. He wanted very much to keep it, since he had already missed the dean's party. He had already prepared the speech— "Democracy in a Crisis"—that he would be delivering to a group of businessmen. Perhaps he might even squeeze in a quick visit with some Ohio relatives. He met his pilot escort, a Lieutenant Coons, in Jacksonville on Friday, February 17. The two-seat army airplane, while not exactly luxurious, would have to suffice. Trubee Davison had really come through for him. They did not leave Jacksonville until nearly 10:30 A.M. because of a blanketing fog. After a refueling stop at Fort Bragg, North Carolina, at 2:30, Coons and passenger Moley headed for southern Ohio.

They never made it.

Coons had no means of communicating with the ground, and, as he headed into thick low clouds, he lost his course. The lieutenant dared not attempt to fly below the cloud deck for fear that the mountainous terrain of western Virginia and northeastern Tennessee was immediately below. To complicate already perilous matters, the sun was beginning to set and their fuel was running low.

Moley feared for his life. If God had spared the nation's president-elect in Miami, maybe the recompense, the Providential quid pro quo, was his closest, most trusted adviser. But at forty-six years of age, with twin eight-year-old boys and a loving wife, Moley had little interest in serving as a cosmic payoff. Besides, he still had an important speech to finish. He and Coons, shouting over the din of the engine, talked about bailing out.

Their big break finally came: a slight opening, a break in the billowy clouds. Coons guided the plane through the slender opening. Farmland was immediately below them; there was nothing left to do but attempt a landing. Coons brought the plane down hard, and the hard earth did not provide much of a cushion as the plane scuttled out of control over the field. It plunged through a wire fence, then into another field, a much softer one. The wheels finally grabbed, and the plane's nose plunged deeply into the Tennessee sod. Coons and Moley looked at each other and burst out laughing. They had tempted death and lived. Somewhere near Maynardville, Tennessee, the professor and the army pilot, shaken but unhurt, disembarked onto the damp soil of a farmer's cornfield. Their plane was destroyed.

The professor did some quick arithmetic: the link between Miami and Maynardville was palpable. What had been a wobbly bench and a brave bystander at Bay Front Park was, two days later, a slight opening in the heavens and a soft field. These chance happenings had somehow conspired to thwart a crazed assassin and a confused pilot. But only a fervently faithful atheist might not see what Moley now saw: the Divine Hand of Fate. Both men had been miraculously spared less than forty-eight hours apart.

More perspective.

Moley (and Roosevelt) could now complete the inaugural address with the gravity and wisdom that the occasion warranted. This could be a heroic speech, a historic speech. It would be, above all else, a Providential speech. Miami and Maynardville had already assured that.

Moley had less than ten days to complete his draft. Roosevelt wanted to meet with him at Hyde Park on February 27 to finalize the speech.

Yet, there was no panic now, no writer's block, as the historic date loomed. Moley was now part of something far bigger, far more transcendent than his own meager resources of invention.

He went back to the desultory draft of February 13. In addition to the page and a half that Miss Pomeranz had typed, Moley had kept his own sloppily handwritten notes on rectangular, hole-punched note cards. He wanted to start anew, but he was not willing to ditch the draft entirely. He particularly wanted to keep some of the material that he had written relating to that most conspicuous of inaugural terms, "dictatorship." Both he and Roosevelt knew that the term could not be invoked in the final draft. It would be too incendiary, too threatening—even if the term was increasingly in circulation as March approached. Moley figured that he had come up with a good cover for the term and, more importantly, the threat it was meant to convey.

but if govt [government] especially in legislative function necessary to introduce new undertakings either fails or delays-there is but 1 [one] recourse & that is to recognize [the] emergency & give wide & clear-cut—even tho [though] temporary authority to executive to put changes into effect—in other words I shall propose to the Cong[ress] a program designed to meet the necessity of an emergency—however great—I shall ask the Congress to enact this program or a program of their own choosing which shall be equally all inclusive & equally sound. But in the event that the Congress shall fail to take 1 [one] of these 2 [two] courses & in the event that at that time the national emergency is still critical I shall ask Cong[ress] for the 1 [one] remaining remedy temporary but broad executive powers to conduct a war against the world emergency just as great as the powers that would be given if we were invaded by a foreign foe.[11]

It was a bit rough, but the threat was strategically and skillfully put forth. In all likelihood, this was a great deal of saber rattling. Moley and Roosevelt knew that they had a clear mandate for a domestic New Deal. They would also have large majorities in both the House and the Senate. Moreover, it also looked increasingly like the lame-duck Congress was going to give the new president broad, if temporary, powers to reorganize the executive branch. No, the suasive force of the statement was aimed less at the Seventy-third Congress than it was toward America's living rooms. Moley and Roosevelt understood that the people would be starved for a program of action after a long season of partisan bickering over what some called the "politics of misery." It was time for some tough, frank talk about depression. It was also time for action. Moreover, just in case Congress felt the slightest inclination for another iteration of the politics of misery, Roosevelt would beat them to the punch. He would commandeer the mandate to lead in his first official act as president on March 4. Rhetorically and politically, it was a brilliant opening. It was also less radical than it actually sounded.

What if Congress simply said "no" to Roosevelt's request for power?

That was not the point. The point was bold, decisive action and to hell with Congress if it could not stomach a program of action. Roosevelt would then constitutionally arrogate to himself war powers. If that was dictatorship, then so be it—although Moley and Roosevelt would leave it to the nation's pundits to draw the inference.

In brief, Moley had found the perfect situational warrant for dictatorship in Congress' failure to act—both the lame-duck Seventy-second Congress, still working on Title IV, and the gun-shy Seventy-third Congress. Public opinion was not far behind. An "economic dictatorship," noted *Literary Digest*, "might not be a bad idea at that, assert many editors. A dictator, they say, might get something done."[12] Moreover, the parallel to war—invasion specifically—was both analogical and metaphorical: The powers that Roosevelt would seek would be akin to those justified by a foreign threat, and he would use such power to wage war against an economic phenomenon. By creating the analogy first, Roosevelt could potentially protect himself from charges of dangerous radicalism. The metaphor therefore followed from the analogy and not vice versa.

Whether Moley had forgotten, or whether he was saving the warfare allusion until later, Roosevelt had created the analogy in their first conversation on the inaugural address back in September. Moreover, back in early November, in the days leading up to Election Day, Roosevelt had increasingly used the analogy of war to talk about his coming administration. At Madison Square Garden on November 5, for example, he acknowledged the "great army" of "loyal voters" who had brought the Democrats "to the gates of victory."[13] Moley was also rhetorically sophisticated enough to recognize that the allusion to war and the allusion to sickness were at loggerheads. A sick nation, a prostrate nation, was not, simultaneously, a fighting nation. Moley and Roosevelt would have to choose.

Moley would also have to choose what to do with all the policies that he had included in his draft written on February 13. As is, the draft looked less like an inaugural address than it did an uninspired laundry list of topics left over from the campaign. This seemed to be the hardest thing for the professor to adjust to: He was no longer writing campaign speeches. As he looked over the topics from his draft—installment buying, reducing taxes, farm and home mortgage relief, transportation policy, and power regulation—he realized how he would have to treat them. The inaugural speech was no time for detailed specifics on the policy front. That could wait until at least March 5, if not the evening of March 4. It was better that they save it for the special legislative session Moley knew Roosevelt was committed to calling. There and then, the nation and its lawmakers could turn their attention to the vexing and potentially contentious arena of policy.

Moley was through with flying—at least for the time being. While Lieutenant Coons, as per military protocol, was forced to return to the crumpled aircraft, Moley was on the train rails, headed for nation's capital. To hell with the speaking engagement in Cincinnati; it had caused all this in the first place. He would meet up with Roosevelt on the evening of the eighteenth back in New York City for the annual meeting of the Inner Circle, a group of New York reporters who trafficked in political lampoon. God only knew that he and Roosevelt could use a few lighthearted moments after what they had been through.

• • •

As the professor wended his way back to Washington, Herbert Hoover was at it again. Instead of telegrams or typed letters, the president wrote to the president-elect in his own hand. Not even his secretaries should know the contents of this letter for fear of what it might do to the nation's financial markets and banks. It was not a short letter. Hoover figured that he had better spell out the details of his eleventh-hour request so that there would be no misunderstandings. He stopped on the tenth page. Unlike the war debts, the forthcoming World Economic Conference, and the ongoing World Disarmament Conference, this situation had more immediate ties to the domestic scene. Even Franklin Roosevelt would be able to see this. Maybe even that asshole Moley would see it, too.

The president was so agitated that he made the most fundamental and elementary of errors: he misspelled the president-elect's last name—twice. He sealed the letter in an envelope and addressed it, "President-Elect Roosevelt." He then placed the envelope into a much larger and heavier brown paper envelope.

W. H. Moran, the chief of the Treasury Department's Secret Service Division, gave John S. West the task of hand delivering the letter to Roosevelt. At 4 P.M. on February 18, West picked up the sealed envelope at the White House from the president's secretary, Lawrence Richey. He then boarded the five o'clock train for New York City. West first stopped off at the Roosevelt residence at 49 East Sixty-fifth Street. Upon learning that the president-elect was attending a banquet at the Hotel Astor, West proceeded there. His Secret Service colleagues had already been instructed to allow him to place the envelope directly in Roosevelt's hands. There could be no intermediaries.

The mission was accomplished at about 11 P.M.

Roosevelt glanced ever so briefly at the letter. He was having a grand time and really wanted to avoid any interruptions. He surreptitiously handed the envelope and letter under the table to Moley, who was astonished to see a letter in the president's own handwriting. He glanced quickly at it. It contained news that he knew had been in the offing for months, but it was news that he had hoped to avoid hearing. He figured it would put a damper on the remaining skits by the Inner Circle.

He figured wrong, however, just as he had figured wrong three days before aboard the *Nourmahal*. Roosevelt continued to enjoy the merriment. He laughed and applauded. He bantered easily and cheerily with those seated nearby. Later, as they moved to exit the ballroom, Roosevelt unhurriedly signed scores of autographs.

Moley again took this to be a fine act on Roosevelt's part. Gravity would surely return when they reached the 49 East Sixty-fifth Street abode. This was, after all, the worst economic news they had received to date. Together with Roosevelt, businessman Basil "Doc" O'Connor, Samuel Rosenman, and Louis Howe, Moley carefully reread the president's letter.

It was a truly remarkable letter. It was remarkable that the president had taken the time and energy to write such a long letter, it was remarkable that the president insinuated blame for the current credit malaise on Roosevelt's November victory, and it was remarkable that Hoover had the temerity to suggest solutions—regarding the currency, the federal budget, taxation, and government credit—that were perfectly in keeping with his own preferred solutions. Above all else, however, the letter was remarkable for its unmistakable emphasis on confidence. Hoover mentioned it explicitly eleven times.[14] In his estimation, the crisis was a crisis of belief: If the people were genuinely fearful, the economic situation would continue to implode. As long as people feared for the security of their money, it would certainly make good sense to withdraw it from their banks. In addition, credit was abundantly available for businesses and banks in the form of loans from the Reconstruction Finance Corporation. Yet, as long as the loans were made public and the public could see firsthand which financial institutions were imperiled, the hoarding of cash and gold would surely continue. It was a self-reinforcing downward spiral: Fear would lead to more fear, which would have material consequences for millions of people.

But Roosevelt could change all of this. If only he would make explicit to the nation what he proposed to do, if only he could give the country prompt assurance that conservative economic policies would be the rule of his administration, this crisis could be cut short. It was all so simple: rhetoric as currency! If only Roosevelt would make public his beliefs, this could stem the tide of deflation and hoarding. Confidence could return. All Roosevelt had to do was state his intentions. No policies. No laws. No presidential proclamations or executive orders. Just words.

It was all so Hooverian. All along, beginning with the stock market crash in October, 1929, the president had pleaded with the American people simply to have confidence in what he was doing. If they believed that the country's economic future would be prosperous, it would in fact be prosperous today. The nation had heard the mantra of confidence for more than three years. Perhaps there should be a public response to this business of confidence, Roosevelt and his advisers figured. But it would have to wait until March 4. The five men agreed that the inaugural address would be a suitable time to address the issue of confidence—and fear, too.

In the meantime, Roosevelt opted for a policy of public silence. He also apparently decided not to write back to the president. It was a most presidential slight.

Hoover, meanwhile, continued to impress upon the incoming administration the need for public assurances in order to facilitate the return of confidence. As Treasury Secretary Ogden Mills prepared to meet with Roosevelt's appointed treasury secretary, Will Woodin, the president reminded Mills that "the causes of this sudden critical development are simple enough. The public is filled with fear and apprehension over the policies of the new administration."[15] The president would have been more accurate had he linked fear and apprehension to the uncertainty of the new administration's policies. Roosevelt had said little publicly about just what economic policies his administration would immediately pursue once in office.

That same day, Wednesday February 22, Hoover said much the same thing in a letter to Pennsylvania senator David A. Reed. The flow of gold out of the country and currency hoarding were both symptomatic of "an alarming state of public mind. That state of mind is simple. It is the breakdown of public confidence in the new administration now coming in."[16] The "only way" for the new administration to reestablish confidence was to disavow inflation by remaining on the gold standard, balance the budget, and avoid overtaxing the federal government's borrowing power.

Hoover, however, was politically astute enough to see just where such assurances would take the Roosevelt administration: "I realize that if these declarations be made by the President- elect, he will have ratified the whole major program of the Republican Administration, that it means the abandonment of 90% of the so-called New Deal." Hoover's 90 percent figure was pure hyperbole: Roosevelt had committed himself repeatedly during the campaign to a balanced budget, economy in government, and what he called a "sound currency." Nonetheless, the president seemed to be writing for posterity, perhaps for a time when the American people would realize the foolishness of their selection and Herbert Hoover might say: "See? I told you so." Even so, if Roosevelt did not commit his administration to these three economic principles, Hoover predicted "a complete financial debacle." If this happened, he wrote in closing the letter to Reed, "the responsibility lies squarely with them for they have had ample warning, unless of course such a debacle is part of the 'new deal.'"

It was a jocular ending, perhaps even ironic. But on February 25, just three days after his letters to Mills and Reed, Hoover had reason to think otherwise about the new administration's intentions. On that day, the president got an urgent memo from Press Secretary Theodore Joslin, who had received an equally urgent telephone call from James H. Rand Jr., president of Remington-Rand, Incorporated. Rand had phoned Joslin shortly after his luncheon meeting with Roosevelt adviser Rex Tugwell, who had bragged openly to Rand that "they [the incoming administration] were fully aware of the bank situation and that it undoubtedly would collapse within a few days, which would thus place the responsibility in the lap of President Hoover. He said we should worry about anything excepting rehabilitating the country after March 4th."[17] Furthermore, Tugwell insisted that once Roosevelt enacted various banking reforms—most notably federal insurance of bank deposits—he would "get credit by all thinking citizens for having saved the day. If nothing is done and collapse happens before March 4th, it will be a calamity and will be blamed on the [Hoover] Administration by Republicans and Democrats alike."

It was a shocking confession of motive. Hoover was justifiably aghast. He wrote to Rand on the twenty-eighth: "When I consider this statement of Professor Tugwell's in connection with the recommendations we have made to the incoming administration, I can say emphatically that he breathes with infamous politics devoid of every atom of patriotism. Mr. Tugwell would project millions of people into hideous losses for a Roman holiday."[18] The president was careful not to state that Roosevelt would engage in such behavior, but it was also clear that he had connected Tugwell's sentiments to the ongoing negotiations, or lack thereof, he was having with the new administration. In other words, ten days after sending the president-elect his lengthy, top-secret epistle, he had heard nary a word from Roosevelt. Not even an acknowledgment of receipt. Tugwell's statement, as reported by Rand, made sense in lieu of this protracted silence.

Now, more than ever, the interregnum politics of recovery was personal. Not only was Roosevelt playing politics at the people's expense, he was also willing to do it at the expense of Herbert Hoover's presidential legacy. The crushing weight of capitalism's failure, or near failure, would accompany Hoover all the way back home to Palo Alto. It might even accompany him beyond the grave. It was most cruel sport.

So, it was with remarkable equipoise and diplomacy that Hoover wrote another handwritten letter to Franklin Roosevelt on February 28. There was nothing shrill in it. No mention was made of the Tugwell remarks. No threats. No hostilities of a personal sort. It was a very tactful, brief, four-paragraph letter. "It is my duty to inform you that the financial situation has become even more grave and the lack of confidence extended further than when I wrote to you on February 18th. I am confident that a declaration even now on the line I suggested at that time would contribute greatly to restore confidence and would save losses and hardships to millions of people."[19]

Hoover, of course, knew in advance what the response would be, but he was not really seeking the president-elect's cooperation. That possibility had died back in January—if not back in April, 1932. Herbert

Hoover was instead writing for posterity. He was writing for his legacy as the nation's thirty-first president. He would remain above the fray. He would salvage his reputation with the American people. They would just have to be patient. But there was also an air of resignation about the letter. Gone were the admonishments to remain on the gold standard, to balance the federal budget, and to maintain the integrity of the government's credit. Hoover instead urged the president-elect "that the co-ordinate arm [Congress] of the government should be in session quickly after March 4th." This was something they could agree on. Beyond calling for a special session of the Seventy-third Congress, Hoover warned that "immediate action may be absolutely essential in the next few days." He would remain faithfully at Roosevelt's "disposal to discuss the situation upon your arrival here or otherwise."

The letter arrived via Secret Service escort at Hyde Park at noon on Wednesday, March 1. By the time the letter reached Roosevelt, the banking situation had grown even graver as worried depositors continued to hoard cash and gold. What had started as an isolated instance of hoarding in Michigan on February 14 had, by month's end, spread like an epidemic across a very credulous nation. Talk of bank closings— "holidays"—was rampant.

As the Secret Service agent waited, Roosevelt dictated a response. Actually, there were two responses. The first letter, Roosevelt claimed, had not been sent because of a misunderstanding with a secretary. It was dated February 20—or was it? Close inspection of the stenographer's handwriting revealed that the day's date had been crossed out and February 20 written in. It appeared to be a retroactive letter, a belated response to Hoover's missive of February 18. It was a diplomatic boner, but Roosevelt was able to cover it up—at least for the time being. In the supposed "early" letter, Roosevelt's tone was remarkably in keeping with Tugwell's lunchtime confessional: "my thought is that it [the banking situation] is so very deep-seated that the fire is bound to spread in spite of anything that is done by way of mere statements. . . . frankly I doubt if anything short of a fairly general withdrawal of deposits can be prevented now."[20] Roosevelt was not only unwilling to try to quench the ravenous flames of fear, he seemed content to let the fire burn itself out. The letter only confirmed Hoover's worst suspicions: The Roman holiday had been ordered and orchestrated from on high.

In the second letter, dated March 1, Roosevelt did not apologize for the delay in sending the supposed earlier letter. He did, however, say that he was "dismayed to find that the enclosed which I wrote in N.Y. a week ago did not go to you, through an assumption by my secretary that it was only a draft of a letter."[21] If by "secretary" Roosevelt was referring to the extremely efficient and reliable Marguerite "Missy" LeHand, Hoover might justifiably have concluded that he was lying. Even so, as Hoover read on, he had to be dismayed: in the brief, three-paragraph letter, Roosevelt had not even addressed the issue of making a public statement on the banking situation. It was as if the request and the situation did not exist—at least not on Hoover's terms. To the president, Roosevelt's protracted and purposeful silence regarding both his letter and his request was irresponsible in the extreme. Yet, Roosevelt had the audacity to speak of a "fine spirit of cooperation" between the two administrations. Hoover had known the president-elect to be a trimmer; he had said as much to Joslin during the campaign. Now, for perhaps the first time, he thought he glimpsed the "real" Roosevelt: a liar, perhaps even a treasonous liar.

It was indeed personal now.

CHAPTER SEVEN

February 27–28, 1933

Ray Moley had no illusions about history. He also harbored no illusions about the historians who would "record" it. As someone who had witnessed the irrepressible Roosevelt charm firsthand, he understood better than most the salutary effects that this charm, this manner, would have on the first generation of Roosevelt historians. Moley also seemed to understand something of the historian's craft. He also knew something of myth.

The evening of February 27, 1933, at Hyde Park was cloudy and cold. A stiff northwest wind swept across the dark waters of the Hudson and tossed the branches of the gaunt old trees around the Roosevelt home. Inside the warm living room a big, thick-shouldered man sat writing by the fire. From the ends of the room two of his ancestors looked down from their portraits: Isaac, who had revolted with his people against foreign rule during an earlier time of trouble, and James, merchant, squire, and gentleman of the old school.

Franklin D. Roosevelt's pencil glided across the pages of yellow legal cap paper: "I am certain that my fellow Americans expect that on my induction into the presidency I will address them with a candor and a decision which the present situation of our Nation impels." The fire hissed and crackled; the large hand with its thick fingers moved rapidly across the page. "The people of the United States want direct, vigorous action. They have made me the instrument, the humble instrument"—he scratched out "humble"; it was not time for humility—"of their wishes."

Phrase after phrase followed in the president-elect's bold, pointed, slanting hand. Slowly, the yellow sheets piled up. By 1:30 in the morning, the inauguration speech was done.[1]

Moley was seventy years old when James MacGregor Burns published this account of what supposedly happened that night. He was not surprised by what he read. Burns had written the professor out of the inaugural address. Not a nod, not a slight gesture—not even an indication that Moley was physically present with Roosevelt as his "thick fingers moved rapidly across the paper." In just eleven years after his death, the first inaugural address had become something of a canonical state paper. If there was a signature Roosevelt text, this was it. If the nation could point to its past and pinpoint the pivotal moment when the Great Depression first looked less formidable, the date would be March 4, 1933. A new spirit had emboldened the enervated nation that day. Even as the words hung in the cold, crisp air of the capital and then moved magically into the nation's living rooms, only to disappear, they seemed to move the country to the very marrow of its collective being.

Rhetorically, spiritually, and politically, the speech had been an unprecedented success. By 1956, it was less a speech than a moment—and Ray Moley had been written out of it. Long before Burns composed his inaugural paean, Franklin D. Roosevelt, the "thick-shouldered" rhetorical savant, had seen to it.

Moley arrived at the family mansion hard by the Hudson on Sunday evening, February 26. In the aftermath of Miami and Maynardville, he had worked assiduously, even reverently, on composing a clean, final draft of the speech. The Hoover letter of February 18 had also provided an inventional impetus.

The draft of the inaugural address was in his briefcase, but it would not remain in his possession for long. Knowing Roosevelt, and knowing how he viewed this occasion and this speech, Moley understood that he would no longer "possess" the speech as of February 28. Rhetorically and materially, it had to be Roosevelt's.

It had to be his in the most fundamental, the most corporeal, of ways. It was not enough simply for Moley to hand over the finished typewritten draft. That would clearly look a bit suspicious to the historians. No, the James MacGregor Burns of the next generation needed something far more dramatic, more mythic—something Providential. At this most crucial and defining hour in the nation's heroic destiny, God would again appear to His people, to the "shining city set upon a hill" so famously articulated by Jonathon Winthrop nearly three centuries earlier.

The nation did not know it this night, would not know it in 1956, but God appeared in the most sentient of forms at Hyde Park in late February: God was Ray Moley. It was a burden he happily surrendered at about 1:30 on the morning of February 28.

Before he could surrender it, however, there was the mundane task of dinner. Shortly after 7 P.M. on Monday, the twenty-seventh, Moley sat down to dinner with Missy LeHand, Roosevelt's ubiquitous and exceedingly "loyal" secretary, a stenographer named Marguerite, and the president-elect. On this most hallowed of evenings, it was curious that the rest of the Roosevelt clan was so conspicuously absent. But perhaps this was a good thing: too many friends and family might interfere with the tranquility that seemed to have descended on Springwood, the name that Roosevelt's dead father James had given the estate. That the president-elect indeed sought tranquility that night is attested to by his after-dinner command: everyone was to head to bed.

At approximately 9 P.M., Roosevelt and Moley moved to the library. Moley brought in his briefcase. Roosevelt sat in a chair that he had found to be particularly comfortable in the executive offices at Albany. The chair was sitting in front of a small folding bridge table. Moley retrieved the draft from his briefcase.

Roosevelt read through it with due deliberation, pausing now and then to exclaim, "that's great!"

At this point, there came an awkward moment: Roosevelt informed the professor that he had better write out the text himself. If the draft were not in his own handwriting, Louis Howe would "have a fit."

Moley knew something of Howe's jealousies. He had seen firsthand several instances when Howe had not only had a "fit" because of others' rhetorical influence, but Moley might well have harkened back to the Democratic National Convention in July—when Roosevelt, Moley, and Samuel Rosenman had carefully crafted the candidate's acceptance speech. They knew that the speech would be Roosevelt's most important to date simply because he was repudiating party tradition by flying to the convention to receive the party's nomination in person.

Howe smelled a rat.

Shortly before the Roosevelt entourage departed from Albany on the way to Chicago, Howe had the speech read to him in its entirety over the phone. He was furious. He could clearly divine, all the way from his musty hotel room at the Commodore Hotel, Rosenman's influence on the speech. Howe, to put it mildly, did not care for "Rosy." Howe grew so incensed with the draft that he immediately began writing an entirely new acceptance speech—despite the fact that he was literally prostrate from fever and chills. He churned out a lengthy speech, which he greeted Roosevelt with as soon as he arrived in Chicago after the eight-hour flight from Albany. As the open-canopied car moved slowly through the cheering throng assembled along Chicago's streets, Howe insisted that Roosevelt use his speech. Sharp words ensued.

"It's much better than the speech you've got now. You can familiarize yourself with it while you ride to the convention hall."

The usually patient Roosevelt momentarily lost his cool: "But dammit Louis, I'm the candidate."[2]

Roosevelt knew immediately that he had gone too far. After all, this was Howe's ultimate moment of political glory—a moment for which he had worked painstakingly for the better part of twenty years. The nominee glanced at the draft as the car moved through the streets. He made a quick decision: He would substitute Howe's first page for the opening of the Roosevelt-Moley-Rosenman speech. It was a brilliant political move. Howe was most pleased as the nation listened to the man who promised them a "new deal."

But Moley knew that Roosevelt's request to draft the speech in his own hand had little if anything to do with Louis Howe. Had he wanted to argue with Roosevelt, Moley could simply have said that the speech would be typed by the time Howe arrived the following morning. Influence would be impossible to determine with a typed manuscript. Moreover, the basic themes in the inaugural address were Roosevelt's anyway.

Moley, however, chose not to argue. He had known before he even got on the train to head north to Hyde Park that Roosevelt would want to redraft the speech in his own handwriting. He was also prepared to impress Roosevelt with one additional gesture of ownership. It would be a page taken right out of the Roosevelt rhetorical playbook.

Before he executed this planned gesture, though, Moley surprised the president-elect with his perspicacity: The professor had even brought appropriate stationery for the occasion, special lined and perforated legal sheets made by the Wilson-Jones office supply company in Newark, New Jersey. The professor could not even get the tablets in New York, so he stocked up at Horders whenever he happened through Chicago.

The drafting began.

Moley sat on a long couch in the library, situated in front of a brightly burning fire. The two went back and forth as they carefully considered the rhetorical choices manifest in each sentence, sometimes in every word. Occasionally they agreed to make a change to Moley's draft. Periodically they would take a break.

During one such break, Moley was overcome by the history in which he clearly recognized he was participating. At 11 P.M., he wrote in his notebook: "Before the fire in the library at Hyde Park. Alone w[ith] F.D.R. He is writing inaugural on a card-table. On the table [a] letter from Lamont with direful warning re[:] banks. Will Woodin calls. Cordell Hull calls. Silence. I am lying on [the] couch. Glasses—whiskey for us. Talk re[:] postal savings banks to care for the people's money." And then Roosevelt broke the solemnity with the question: "How do you spell foreclose?"[3]

Moley waxed historic. "A week—yes five days—this man will be Pres[ident] of U.S." He closed his brief note with "A strong man F.D.R."

It all seemed so incredible to the professor. Here he was helping the next president of the United States draft one of the most important inaugural addresses in the history of the Republic—in his library, sipping his whiskey, lying on his couch, and sharing intimate thoughts on the future of the nation. Indeed, he had come a long way from Olmsted Falls, Ohio—a very, very long way. The distance, the proximity—ground zero of history, the incredible influence, and the booze—it was enough to make a professor feel a bit light in the head.

Roosevelt continued writing. As 1:30 in the morning on Tuesday approached, Moley informed the president-elect that he had purposefully omitted a peroration. He figured that Roosevelt would want to have the last word for his inaugural address. It should be personal. It should invoke the Deity. Roosevelt, picking up on the suggestion, scribed: "In this dedication of a nation we humbly ask the blessing and the guidance of God. May he protect each and every one of us. May he guide me in the days to come."[4] Before he signed his name at the end of page ten, Roosevelt crossed out "and the guidance." The nation needed "blessings." He would reserve God's guidance for himself.

The address was now finished, nearly four and a half hours after they had begun. Moley had been anticipating—and choreographing—this moment of closure. It needed something grand, something dramatic, perhaps some gesture to empower the new author of the speech.

Moley rose slowly from the couch and deliberately gathered the pages of the draft that he had brought with him to Hyde Park, the pages that Roosevelt had so painstakingly copied. He approached the glowing embers of the fire and tossed the pages into the fireplace. They were quickly consumed. Moley turned to the future president and said, "This is your speech now."[5]

What Roosevelt did not know, what James MacGregor Burns and a generation of his cohorts did not know, is that Ray Moley kept most of his notes. Perhaps the speech would again someday be his.

By March 4, Moley understood that the nation's anticipation for the speech would be palpable, and it was not just about the economic situation or the increasingly grave banking matter. Yes, the nation would be terribly concerned about unemployment and hoarding, and what Roosevelt might propose to address those problems, but that anticipation seemed to pale compared to the silence, the mystery, engendered by Roosevelt's carefully cultivated persona during the four-month interregnum. The president-elect had made no major speeches, certainly none that were broadcast to the nation. He had voiced his agreement or his dissent with the Hoover administration and its attempts to bring him on board with great circumspection, if not studied ambiguity. For all intents and purposes, Roosevelt remained a cipher. From Emporia, Kansas, an exasperated William Allen White spoke for many: "No one knows his heart and few have seen behind the masking smile that wreathes his face. We have had to be satisfied with urbanity when we needed wisdom, with mystery when we should have a complete understanding. We are putting our hands in a grab-bag. Heaven only knows what we shall pull out."[6]

This is not to say that the president-elect had become a recluse. On the contrary, Roosevelt, right up until his departure from Hyde Park on March 1, was extremely visible to the public. He just did not say much. Then again, the upward thrust of the jaw, the frequently raised fedora, the jaunty angle of the cigarette holder, and that toothy Roosevelt smile alerted the nation that he would be no Herbert Hoover. He would not succumb to the specter of capitalism's demise—nor would he take on its physiognomy of despair. What remained to be seen was just how Roosevelt would attempt to turn the tide against the Great Depression. Then again, perhaps the answer was already apparent in his outwardly confident body language.

His campaign speeches were of little help. Throughout his trips across the country, Roosevelt had swung left, then right, then seemingly left again. It was all very confusing—and frustrating—for the traveling press who expected some degree of consistency. By November, the editors of the liberal weekly the *Nation* were exasperated: "if anybody can get a clear-cut view of Governor Roosevelt's fundamental principles, his deep and underlying beliefs, he is much cleverer than we."[7]

Roosevelt's silence on policy after the election only exacerbated the uncertainty of what his administration might do. What did he mean by a "sound, but adequate, currency"? What did he mean by making the tariff "effective"? Did he really favor a "general withdrawal of deposits"? Would he mirror the actions of many governors and declare a banking "holiday"? How could he balance the budget while favoring a broad program of public works? How could he excoriate the Hoover administration for its profligate spending while proclaiming that the "day of enlightened administration" had dawned? How would he continue to separate war debts from world disarmament and the forthcoming London Economic Conference? And what of confidence, that intangible so fundamental to economics and banking? Would he laud it, as he had at Columbus in August, or would he ignore it as mere Hooverian pap? In sum, he needed to communicate some measure of control, some degree of reassurance in the inaugural address.

Using a pencil, Roosevelt began, in his best handwriting, to set the tone of the speech: "I am certain that my fellow Americans expect that on my induction to the Presidency I will address them with a candor and a decision which the present situation of our nation impels."[8] It was a most interesting opening statement. In a moment of such overwhelming uncertainty, the three opening words, "I am certain," were most appropriate—and most reassuring. But there was also a curious remove, a distance, communicated in this opening sentence. Why did Moley and Roosevelt favor the less immediate "fellow Americans" and "them" with something much more proximate? What had happened to the second person? There was also the distance of a metalevel statement. That is, Roosevelt was already rehearsing, just a few words into his very first presidential act, his audience's expectations about inaugural speechmaking. Roosevelt was not engaged in some sort of sophisticated rhetorical criticism; rather, the words, the expectations, were identificatory. He did not even have to say it: he and his audience were in lockstep just thirty-three words into the speech.

Moley and Roosevelt had raised the question of speaking, specifically genre and its expectations. Just what sort of inaugural address would this be? It would not aim at transcendence. No, the situation was much too grave for high-minded, far-removed principles. The times needed candor and decision, truth telling and action. Franklin Roosevelt and his constituents could not afford the luxury of abstraction and contemplation typical of so many of his predecessors' opening-day words. To make the point further about the generic requirements of the moment, Roosevelt and Moley wrote, "This is no occasion for soft speaking or for the raising of false hopes." Another metalevel statement about presidential speechmaking, although this one was aimed at the man who would be seated in the big leather chair to Roosevelt's immediate left. Just one sentence into the address, Moley and Roosevelt raised the issue of Hoover's penchant to equate presidential speech with presidential policy. Moreover, Roosevelt would not explicitly engage in the economics of confidence, nor would he speak around the issues confronting the nation on March 4.

Read against the backdrop of the season of silence, the long and arduous four months of partisan bickering, grave fear, and uncertainty, the rhetorical persona crafted in the first paragraph was remarkable. Roosevelt was certain; he knew the occasion and the audience's expectations; he would tell the truth, regardless of consequence; he was decidedly not Herbert Hoover. And, of no small importance, he was not "soft." This last assurance was not without consequence during the primary season and the fall general election. He had frequently been attacked in public and private as being "weak," or, in the words of one Hoover insider, a "pussyfooter," a real "lady" in a most "ladylike" affair.[9] His crippled condition was understood by many in strictly gendered terms: to be unable to walk on his own, to be dependent for his locomotion on others was a most effeminate condition. It was decidedly "soft." Yet, in the first paragraph of his first presidential speech, Roosevelt and Moley gave testimony to the speaker's hardihood, his "hardness" in the face of the most grave of situations, his full and uncompromised masculinity.

It was a most curious beginning to a new administration, a sort of primer on generic requirements for inaugural addresses—and why

Franklin Roosevelt was going to break them. At another level, the speech might reassure the thousands watching and listening and the millions listening and imagining, that their new president was plenty "hard." America's most phallic institution would not be compromised by four more years of Hooverian limpness. In brief, it was perhaps a most untraditional start for a day that celebrated democracy's most prized tradition of the orderly transfer of executive power.

There was also no talk of fear, or of fearing fear. There was nothing overtly rhetorical about this unusual opening. No antithesis. No parallelism. No alliteration or assonance. Not even an overt metaphor.

Moley and Roosevelt had to be careful, though. A situation singularly unique in the history of the republic could frighten more than reassure. Speaking requirements—genres—were comfortable and reassuring things, after all. There were two important precedents, however. Both involved wars. Both invoked near-mythic events and mythic leaders. "In the crisis of our War for Independence in the poverty, the unrest and the doubts of the early days of constitutional government, in the dark days of the War between the States, a leadership of frankness and vigor has met with that understanding and support of the people themselves which is an essential to victory." Moley and Roosevelt opted for analogy, not metaphor. The metaphor of sickness had clearly lost out to the analogy of war. The "sick nation in the midst of a sick world" had given way to heroic origins and the nation's defining trial in the span of two weeks. Yes, wars invoked death, dying, and suffering, but they also bound the incipient and the internecine in ways that an ahistorical sickness never could.

But the point Moley and Roosevelt seemed intent on making was not metaphorical. The nation was not privy to the rough draft. The analogy instead was about a style of leadership and the role of the people. The leadership of a Washington and a Lincoln commanded the nation's assent. Extraordinary times meant extraordinary executive actions, and this meant a willingness on the people's part to acquiesce, albeit temporarily, to a more singular or concentrated form of leadership. Already Moley and Roosevelt were looking to the latter stages of the speech where, again, the analogy of war would be invoked to inform executive actions. "Dictatorship." Or, was it "dictatorial powers"?

What bound the nation together was less its common history, its defining hours of war, than the support the people were willing to invest in their leaders. Not its institutions, but its leaders. Although Moley and Roosevelt had no illusions about a de facto inheritance of the Washington and Lincoln mantels, the aim was to inherit broadminded constituents. That inheritance was a duty, a living obligation, enforced by a single little linking verb. The nation's past—its birth and near death—was a living past. The leadership needed in those days was not in the past; that leadership "*has* met" not "had met," not even just "met." It was a living obligation that Moley and Roosevelt were attempting to evoke, an obligation that, if refused, could also rewrite the nation's understanding of its collective past. This was a most solemn obligation—so solemn that it was assumed, not solicited.

Then there was the matter of "a leadership of frankness and vigor." Would the nation notice the pun? Would they see through to the "Frank-ness" of Franklin's vigor? Probably not. It could stay for now.

The candor mentioned in the opening sentence returned in the third paragraph. Rather than bury the nation's maladies in the middle of the speech, Moley and Roosevelt placed them firmly at the front end, thereby enacting the type of forthright speech stipulated from the outset. In his earlier outlines of the address, Moley had placed "the failures" immediately after the opening allusion to "sick nations." By February 27, however, Moley and Roosevelt had changed the wording—away from the unqualified "failure" to a much more palatable "common difficulties." They parsed further: the initial listing of difficulties would be "on the side of material things." The parsing had two rhetorical functions: It allowed, even encouraged, the specification of blame while at the same time serving again to draw a contrast with Hoover's belief that the material and the immaterial were inseparable.

The list was comprehensive: prices had declined, taxes had risen, budgets had not been balanced, wages had shrunk, trade had stopped, farmers had no markets for their produce, great numbers of people were unemployed, and the savings of thousands of families had disappeared.

This was indeed a leadership of candor. Rather than vague generalities of the depression's severity, Moley and Roosevelt opted for explicit detail. Perhaps the reason why they favored this rhetorical approach punctuates the severity: "Only a foolish optimist can deny the dark realities of the moment." Not only was this an outright condemnation of Hoover, it was also a bold indictment of his rhetorical emphasis on confidence and optimism. It was a bold gesture—perhaps even partisan—but Moley and Roosevelt were certain that the nation would recognize the person and the pattern being condemned.

To ensure listeners understood that the fault clearly belonged to Hoover and his brethren in the Republican Party, they further emphasized the rhetoric of confidence in paragraph six: "Our national distress comes from no failure of substance. We are stricken by no plague of locusts." The statement offered a radical reversal of Moley and Roosevelt's earlier plans to stress sickness, perhaps as a cause and certainly as a consequence. No, the nation seemed perfectly healthy. Nor had some sort of Providential quid pro quo for years of greed caused famine or starvation. This was not about God—not about this part of the "distress" anyway. At a thoroughly secular level, "Nature still offers her bounty and human efforts have multiplied it." The blame lay clearly with "the rulers of the exchanges of mankinds' goods," whose "stubborness" and "incompetence" and allegiance to "outworn tradition" had not brought the nation's economy out of a virtual standstill. These same "rulers" had, within two paragraphs, become the "money changers," the men who Christ expelled from the temple for defiling holy ground. Roosevelt was particularly pleased with the phrase, "The philosophy of the money changers stands indicted in the court of public opinion, rejected by the hearts and minds of men." He had come up with it while attending Sunday services at Saint James Episcopal Church the day before.

Moley and Roosevelt had done a smart thing: They were giving the people a group to blame, but without naming any names. Both knew that if the nation's economy were to improve after March 4, bankers, industrialists, investors, and entrepreneurs of all stripes would be needed in the effort. Moreover, their guilt was not infused with evil designs. They had "tried," but they were too constrained by tradition. The one person who may have been identifiable in all of this—Herbert Hoover—would soon be leaving town anyway. As if to specify that the principal villain was the outgoing president, Moley and Roosevelt for the third time invoked his favorite solution: "Faced by failure of the lure of profit, they have resorted to exhortations pleading tearfully for restored confidence." Hoover's mantra was being transformed into Roosevelt's evidentiary, if lachrymose, mantra.

The other smart thing that Moley and Roosevelt had done was to avoid specifying exactly what had caused the Great Depression. All they were doing was blaming some vaguely unspecified group for trying to solve the problem, but failing. The cause seemed to lie with a series of actions rather than with a group of people. Callousness, selfishness, the mad chase for profits, money without work—these were the actions that had caused so many problems. Thus, restoring the nation to the "ancient truths" would require a change in values. Without the recognition of the "moral stimulation of work," and the "joy of creative effort," confidence could never return. Here, finally, was Rooseveltian confidence: "it thrives only on honesty, on honor, on the sacredness of obligations, on faithful protection, on unselfish performance. Without them it cannot live." More importantly, confidence could not be manufactured out of thin air, out of the epiphenomenon of mere words that a president articulated, as if by some sort of magical incantation.

At some point between February 13 and 27, Moley had dropped the esoteric idea that the nation's collective economic failure was a matter simply of "mechanics & method." Regardless of its truth, the nation did not want to hear its president, on inauguration day, drone on about the machine age, productive capacity outstripping consumption, and other arcane institutional explanations. The nation did not need another "Great Engineer" quite so soon. It needed a story with drama, with heroes and villains, easy explanations and archetypes—all wrapped up in a memorable style.

The story also needed some resolution, lest depression hold sway for another four years. In his very first outline for the inaugural address, between points number five—the good neighbor—and six—

dictatorship—Moley had penned "action needed." It was the only thing underlined on the page. Now, as Roosevelt finished writing on the page, he left a long blank space on the legal pad. Perhaps he and Moley planned to go back and say more about confidence. More likely, they wanted to start the transition to "action and action now" with a fresh, new page. The main task before the country was simply putting people to work. Rather than the detailed list that Moley had put together on the evening of the thirteenth, however, the "actions" were now conflated into single anaphoric sentences. Action would involve public works, rebalancing the population between industrial centers and farms, raising the value of agricultural products, mortgage relief for farmers and homeowners, reducing governmental costs, unifying relief activities, better national planning, better supervision of public utilities, supervision of banks and exchanges, and a sound currency. These measures constituted the new administration's "lines of attack," which Roosevelt would bring before the Congress meeting in special session. Roosevelt punctuated the details of the forthcoming legislative session by leaving two-thirds of the fifth page blank. He and Moley next turned to the thorny matter of international affairs.

Moley had become something of an autodidact on the intricacies of foreign policy and international economics. In the wake of Roosevelt's invitation to the first White House conference with Hoover and Mills back on November 22, Moley had but precious few days to understand the mysterious mechanics of Old World politics, diplomacy, and finance. It was a daunting task, but the professor had managed to hold his own against the venerable treasury secretary and the nonpareil expertise of the president. Moley's crash course might have been averted had his candidate decided to make foreign relations an issue during the fall campaign, but Roosevelt and his inner circle decided against it. Hoover was not campaigning on the issue, and Roosevelt making a speech on the subject raised the very real likelihood of a Stimson retort. Raising the ire of the august secretary of state was to be carefully avoided.

Nevertheless, the nation still needed to know what its new leader proposed to do in the increasingly important realm of foreign affairs.

Did he, like Hoover, propose to internationalize the depression—at the level of both causes and solutions?

The answer seemed to lie in the preceding paragraph, or the "lines of attack": The new president would commit himself to calling for an immediate special session of Congress. Moley had argued passionately with Roosevelt at various points during the interregnum not to adopt Hoover's proposals to internationalize the depression via war debts, the economic conference, or the ongoing disarmament talks. The logic, to Moley, was simple: take advantage of a receptive and massively Democratic Congress to push through important measures aimed at economic recovery. A hostile Congress, a Congress divided by the rancor that protracted foreign affairs negotiations would inevitably engender, should be scrupulously avoided. The New Deal—the *domestic* New Deal—hung in the balance.

In the end, Moley's side had won, but by how much he did not know. Perhaps he did not even want to know. Whatever the case, the professor could perhaps rub it in a bit on inauguration day. Earlier, he had alluded to Lincoln and the war over which he had presided. Now, he invoked Lincoln's rhetorical legacy: "Through this program of action we address ourselves to putting our own national house in order. Our international trade relations, though vastly important, are in point of time and necessity secondary to the establishment of a sound national economy." Lincoln's divided house was now whole again, but conservatively inclined bankers, financiers, and other Wall Street elites sought to repair it from the outside in. Roosevelt proposed to move in the opposite direction, though not defiantly: "I shall spare no effort to restore world trade by international economic readjustment but the emergency at home cannot wait on that accomplishment." It was time to begin the repair work from the inside out.

Moley and Roosevelt decided to extend the imagery of the home even farther. The American home was not an isolated outpost, or what they termed "narrowly nationalistic." No, the nation, echoing Roosevelt's "Concert of Interests" speech delivered at Oglethorpe University in May, would recover economically only if it recognized "the interdependence of the various elements in and parts of the United

States." The nation could not survive half-boom and half-bust. Lincoln again.

A few weeks earlier, Moley had been working on possible inserts to the speech, catchy ideas and statements that might crystallize a philosophy of governance, an ideal of citizenship. The professor had noted one such idea in early February, on the train ride from Warm Springs to Jacksonville. With Ed Flynn and Roosevelt brainstorming, he later penned "the good neighbor." Weeks later, he attempted an elaboration. He began one such insert thus: "He resolutely respects himself. He respects the rights of others."[10] The "he" in question was a good citizen, the type of person who would "not if he can help it be a public charge when the community falls into depression." Moley and Roosevelt now transferred some of that language into a much larger "community," but a community all the same. "In the field of world policy I would dedicate this nation to the policy of the good neighbor—the neighbor who resolutely respects himself and because he does so respects the rights of others—the neighbor who respects his obligations and respects the sanctity of his agreements in and with a world of neighbors." The "he" of Moley's ideal America had, in the span of a few weeks, become less an economic being and more of a benign diplomat. He was a neighbor who did not give a damn about what might happen inside the neighborhood gulag or crematorium as long as his lawn was not trespassed or trod asunder. He was also a neighbor who cared a great deal about war debts, particularly those that were owed him by England and France. He was a neighbor who was not ready to trade his World War I IOUs, "his agreements," for nonpecuniary concessions. The war debts had to be paid. Europeans needed to know they could not fight future wars with American dollars repayable on whatever terms they chose. No, the war debts needed to be a living obligation, not a bargaining chip to be casually tossed around at the diplomatic table.

Here were the residual hostilities that Moley harbored with the likes of Stimson, Davis, Mills, and Hoover. The good neighbor gestured abroad, but perhaps more importantly, he was defining new terms of conduct within his own house. With this vaguely worded but emphatic articulation, Roosevelt closed page seven. His transition back to domestic matters was again signaled by a lengthy blank space between pages seven and eight. It would be the final transition of the inaugural address. It would prove to be an ominous lacuna. In the long history of presidential inaugural speeches, only Lincoln's first could rival its gravity. And, like Lincoln's, the term that bound the section together was warfare.

It was certainly not a novel term as applied to the Great Depression; Hoover had been using it for the better part of three years. What was novel was the extent to which Moley and Roosevelt now decided to ramify the term to make it more effective. Where it could count most, they figured, was at the executive level, where decisive leadership could most effectively be marshaled to wage such a war. It was a leadership that Herbert Hoover had carefully avoided, perhaps even abdicated. His "war on a thousand fronts" was a highly fragmented war, fought by counties and localities. The war had yet to be nationalized. The nation remained to be unified. In July, at the Democratic National Convention, following Roosevelt's dramatic flight to Chicago to receive the nomination in person, he had declared that the campaign was "more than a political campaign; it is a call to arms."[11] Now elected, he and Moley would make that call effective.

To do so, they returned to the beginning. The word that Moley had suggested in September at the Palace Hotel in San Francisco returned: "Our people, now inured to hardship and suffering, do not fear the rigors of *discipline*. They are, I know, ready and willing to submit their lives and property to a *discipline* which aims clearly and honestly at a larger good." It was a remarkable assumption, belied perhaps by the fact that it was delivered to a third person. Here was an important rhetorical flaw: If such discipline was going to be assumed, if a sacrifice involving lives and property was going to be invoked, it simply had to be more personal. That flaw would be corrected by March 4. On February 27, Roosevelt continued in the impersonal idiom: "This I propose to offer *them*, pledging to *them* that the larger purposes will bind upon us all as a sacred obligation, with a unity of duty heretofore evoked only in times of armed strife." It was an impersonal pledge, and it would be the second pledge taken within the hour. The first pledge—the oath of office—would involve three people: Chief Justice Charles Evans Hughes, Franklin Roosevelt, and God. The nation would act only as a passive witness. By contrast, in the inaugural address, Roosevelt would enter into his own sacred pledge with the American people. But it was not a solitary pledge; it was a pledge that would bind them together in the most solemn of ways.

First and foremost, the pledge was transformative. It meant something immediately. It was exactly the sort of action they hoped to inaugurate. "With this pledge taken, I assume unhesitatingly the sword of leadership of an army dedicated to a disciplined attack upon our common problems." There was that word "discipline" again. Far more important, though, was the transformation that occurred: In just one declarative sentence, the "people" had become a disciplined and dedicated "army." Rhetorically, the move was brilliant: The pledge now bound the people to their new president with a "sacred" bond. Roosevelt's audience would also take an oath on inaugural day, and it was not just a civic oath carried out in front of ordinary witnesses. No, this was an oath of Providential import; witnessed by God. To ignore this call would be worse than treason, it would be the far more grave offense of sacrilege. Moreover, Roosevelt's army would be conspicuously and purposefully singular; there would be no thousand armies fighting on a thousand different fronts. It would indeed, as the new president promised, constitute "a *unity* of duty."

As the speech neared a close, some of the language and form of Moley's first drafts resurfaced. For example, Moley and Roosevelt agreed to use the phrase "a stricken nation in the midst of a stricken world." The professor had begun an earlier draft of the speech with "We are a sick nation in the midst of a sick world." The emphasis on "stricken" was much more ambiguous than "sick," and it allowed Roosevelt to acknowledge the severity of the moment without being maudlin or overly morose about it. Nor would the image of sickness comport with an active army. Moreover, a stricken nation would require an active, vigorous leader—a fighter, not a doctor. His symbol of leadership would be a sword, not a stethoscope.

One other phrase also returned. Weeks earlier, in his final outline, Moley had written, "no essential failure of democ[racy]," which was a slight revision of "no failure of Dem[ocracy]." As the hour passed midnight, Roosevelt wrote, "We do not distrust the future of essential democracy." A reassurance originally expressed in the past tense now moved to the future tense. But the assurance was ominous: Why qualify democracy with "essential"? What was "nonessential" to democracy that Roosevelt might not trust? The "failure" of an earlier draft was now reassigned to cover another phrase on Moley's final outline, "tribute to people." The draft now read, "the people of the United States have not failed." This was not much of a tribute, but it would have to suffice.

Moley and Roosevelt also decided to keep nearly verbatim a paragraph that the professor had drafted on February 13. It was an aggrandizing paragraph, perhaps overly dramatic, but the two men knew that it would work with the American audience. It was bold, confrontational, and they amended the original only slightly: "But in the event that the Congress should fail to take one of these two courses, and in the event that the national emergency is still critical, I shall not evade or quit. I shall ask the Congress for the one remaining instrument to meet the crisis—broad Executive powers to wage a war against the world." Roosevelt quickly crossed out the word *world* and picked up with "emergency as great as the power that would be given me if we were in fact invaded by a foreign foe." He seemed pleased with what he had just written, so much so that he went back to the term *But*. Next to it, he penciled in a mark denoting a new paragraph. This statement should stand alone.

The changes that Moley and Roosevelt made to the February 13 paragraph were subtle but important. First, Moley's original formulation contained only one first-person reference. Now it contained three direct, personal references. If Congress shirked its duty, Roosevelt would seek to consolidate his authority under the aegis of war. He again was working rhetorically at the level of analogy, not metaphor, and the power exerted presumably would be legal and material rather than rhetorical. The power, in contrast to earlier drafts, would not be dictatorship, because Roosevelt would have to ask for such executive powers from Congress. That said, the sentiment was decisive, bold, and personal. A dictator might have mouthed such a sentiment. Moreover, Congress would be on high alert: the nature of the analogy meant that not to act would be akin to high treason.

A second key change to the original wording involved the term *instrument*. Moley had originally used the phrase "the 1 [one] remaining remedy." To use the term *remedy,* though, was to invoke the image of a prostrate people, a sick people. Just as a "sick nation" had been changed to a "stricken nation," so too had Moley and Roosevelt decided to use a more neutral, less enervating term. Thus, instrument.

But what was this instrument? Was the instrument really about declaring war? Did Moley and Roosevelt cue their listeners how to interpret the term just four sentences hence? "They [the American people] have asked for discipline and direction under leadership. They have made me the instrument, the temporary humble instrument, of their wishes." To make matters even more suggestive, on November 7, 1932, in his last public utterance before Election Day, Roosevelt had waxed nostalgic to his neighbors gathered in Poughkeepsie. "Favor comes because for a brief moment in the great space of human change and progress some general human purpose finds in him a satisfactory embodiment." Roosevelt continued, "To be the means through which the ideal and hopes of the American people may find a greater realization calls for the best in any man. I seek to be only the humble emblem of this restoration."[12] In less than four months, the "humble emblem" had become the "humble instrument." Thus had perhaps the executive and executive powers come to be represented in just one instrument: Franklin Roosevelt. It was a decidedly nonhumble instrument. James MacGregor Burns was right in his thinking but wrong on the history: humble would not be crossed out. Not yet.

Third, Moley and Roosevelt deleted the word *world;* this would remain a domestic emergency.

Fourth, the phrase "temporary but broad executive powers" was rewritten as the clock neared one. It now read simply, "broad Executive powers." Who knew how long this war would last?

Finally, at 1:30 in the morning on Tuesday, February 28, the president-elect signed his name on page ten to signify that the inaugural address was now completely drafted—and that it was now his.

Shortly afterward, his dramatic act of incineration complete, Ray Moley headed to the guest bedroom for some much-needed sleep. He took his briefcase with him. It contained his claim upon "history."

CHAPTER EIGHT

February 28–March 3, 1933

Roosevelt had of course been right: Upon his arrival at Hyde Park on Tuesday, February 28, Louis Howe did indeed want to have a careful look at the inaugural address. Over the course of the next twenty-four hours, there would be no small debate at Springwood as to what the speech should look like on March 4.

Moley was not terribly concerned about Howe's rhetorical interventions. Unlike Samuel Rosenman, he had always gone the extra mile to include the sensitive Howe in all phases of his work. Moreover, Moley also understood that any influence he had with the president-elect was bound up with his relationship with Howe. It was Howe, after all, who had recruited the professor into the governor's wide circle of advisers in the first place. As he headed south, back to his apartment, Moley was not worried about possible changes to the speech.

His lack of concern was also buttressed by Roosevelt's phone call later that day. In their conversation, he informed Moley that Howe had dictated all of his handwritten draft to the stenographer, changing in all about fifty words. That was vintage Louis, Moley thought, always wanting to have a hand, no matter how small, in The Boss's big moments. Roosevelt assured the professor that he would change Howe's amendments back to their original wording.[1]

Whether Roosevelt was fibbing to Moley or whether Howe was fibbing to Roosevelt, suffice it to say that more than a mere fifty words was involved in Louis Howe's changes. At stake were more than 350 words—mostly additions. This was not just a minor stylistic cleanup. Moley did not know this, of course, and he would see the true extent of Howe's interventions until the evening of March 1. Nevertheless, Howe's influence did not worry him. If any one of the president-elect's advisers had Roosevelt's best interests in mind, it was Howe. Besides, Moley knew that Howe could edit, and edit well. A lifelong newspaperman, the sixty-one-year-old Howe had cultivated the skill for more than forty years.

He could not say the same salutary things for others of the president-elect's intimates. Moley was particularly miffed at Rex Tugwell, who kept trying to make suggestions for the inaugural address. In fact, on February 24, the day before Tugwell sent Hoover apoplectic with his cavalier confessions to James Rand Jr., Moley had had enough. Instead of listening patiently to his Columbia University colleague's suggestions, Moley did the one thing the loquacious Tugwell would understand: he said nothing and walked away. Why was it that so many of Roosevelt's advisers thought themselves rhetoricians when they found out about Moley's speechwriting duties? The professor had long before grown weary of the rhetorical diplomacy.

When he arrived in New York City, Moley had other immediate concerns—like his physical safety. Maynardville and Miami had clearly heightened matters of security and safety for the professor. Now he was informed of something most peculiar: a small, clearly disturbed Italian man had been seen outside his residence. Later, his assistant, Celeste Jedel, had seen the man outside his office. She reported that the man had asked to see Moley, claiming he had drawings to show him of the office window and its relationship to the office entrance. This being the two-week "anniversary" of the Zangara assassination attempt, Moley could not be too careful: police were immediately dispatched to monitor the movements of the "little incoherent Italian." Police were also immediately dispatched to Santa Barbara, California, to watch over his twin sons. Fortunately, blueprints and not bullets were the extent of this other Italian's vexations.

Back at Hyde Park, another little man was engaged in a most important "dictation." Howe fancied himself, perhaps even above his considerable skills as a political operative, an artist—a poet, a painter, a playwright. He now brought that talent to bear on what would be one of the most highly anticipated speeches in the nation's history.

It is a rare moment in time when expectations of a high order are actually met, let alone exceeded, when the fevered pitch of anticipation finds fulfillment in the transcendent. It is altogether doubtful whether Howe entertained such thoughts as he began his dictation, yet with one phrase Howe would capture the essence of a man and an age.

He found Moley and Roosevelt's introduction pinched, too hurried. If the president was truly serious about addressing the nation "with a candor and a decision," why not do it from the outset? And why start with a negative statement? Why not begin on a positive note rather than saying, "This is no occasion for soft speaking or for the raising of false hopes"? Howe opted for something bold, something positive, even if touched with a tinge of legalism. "This is preeminently the time to speak the truth, the whole truth frankly and boldly."[2] It was still a meta-statement, a statement about the very act of speaking, but at least it was positive. Speaking "frankly and boldly"—this would be enacted throughout the speech's duration.

Then came a most reassuring promise: "This great nation will endure as it has endured will revive and will prosper." By making this promise, Roosevelt would enter the genealogy of the nation's leaders. Only the president could give meaningful expression and embodiment to such a statement. The "endurance" would not be premised nor promised in law; it would not be the perpetuity of union argument made so forcefully and eloquently by the nation's sixteenth president in his first inaugural address. The future of the nation for Lincoln was vouchsafed by the accretion of law: the Articles of Association, the Declaration of Independence, the Articles of Confederation, and finally the Constitution itself. The future of the nation in 1933 relied on something far more potentially ephemeral, maybe even, God forbid, ineffable. "So first of all let me assert my firm belief that the only thing we have to fear is fear itself—nameless, unreasoning, unjustified terror which paralyzes the needed effort to bring about prosperity once again." By 1933, seventy-two years to the day after the melancholy Lincoln promised a future based on law, that promise was bankrupt. A union of legalism promised no sustenance to a starving nation. The calcified words on a page, the principled promise of Lincoln, were shorn of relevance. Little wonder the nation bubbled with expectant talk of the decidedly un-Lincolnian "dictatorship."

Fear—regardless of how Louis Howe freighted it with ominous specifics—had brought the nation to perhaps its most direful day. Or was it terror? Was that not what Herbert Hoover had been saying for three years? How could a president pin the "endurance" of the country on a statement that, logically speaking, made no sense? Where did Howe come up with such a striking sentiment?

Roosevelt clearly liked Howe's introductory handiwork. At some point on March 1, he had read Howe's revisions and made a few changes of his own. The only thing Howe had gotten wrong with the fear statement was that he had ended it on too narrow of a note. "The only thing we have to fear is fear itself" should not be limited solely to an economic locus, "to bring about prosperity once again." The president-elect moved to make the statement metaphorically consistent with the back half of the address. In his distinctive and choppy admixture of the block and the cursive, he wrote above the crossed out section, "needed efforts to convert retreat into advance." In his postpolio rhetoric, Roosevelt fancied himself as the peripatetic leader. As such, he needed to counter the word *paralyzes* with a more mobile, more vigorous sentiment.

Of the many changes Howe made, Roosevelt vetoed outright only a few. One such veto involved the natural imagery that Moley and he had earlier used to characterize trade and industrial enterprise. In their February 27 draft, the two decided to use imagery that Moley had developed in early February, thus: "The means of exchange are frozen in the currents of trade; the leaves of industrial enterprise are withered." Howe did not like the benign naturalism, the lack of human agency in the statement. He dictated, "the means of exchange are being timidly herded and diverted *from* the currents of trade; industrial enterprise is stagnate." Although the statement had a nice cadence to it, even rhythm, the president-elect overrode his longtime confidante. The statement could plausibly be read as an indictment of the American people for hoarding vast sums of cash and gold as the banking crisis grew graver by the hour. The key preposition, the one that Howe had gotten wrong, was "from."

Roosevelt crossed out the text and inserted, "the means of exchange are frozen *in* the currents of trade; the withered leaves of industrial enterprise lie on every side." By replacing "from" with "in," Roosevelt rekindled the sentiment that he was talking about world trade, about products *in* transit, and not a domestic hoarding that kept products *from* the currents of trade. The president-elect had also changed, however subtly, the wording that he and Moley had agreed upon. The February 27 draft had effectively left the leaves on the tree—withered, not dead. By March 1, those same leaves had fallen from the tree of enterprise.

Howe made another change that Roosevelt also vetoed. This one was less obvious, but it was perhaps even more important than frozen currents and withered leaves. In his dictation, Howe had left intact the reference in the second paragraph to the "War for Independence," the early days of "constitutional government," and the "dark days of the war between the states." This was a statement of continuity and genealogy. What Howe did change was a verb tense: "a leadership of frankness and vigor *met* with that understanding and support of the people themselves which is essential to victory." Howe had clearly missed the nuance. Between the terms *vigor* and *met,* Roosevelt reinserted the term *has.* That past was a living past, one that the president would inherit even as he called on it to animate the present.

Howe also changed the all-important paragraph near the close of the speech where Moley and Roosevelt had constituted the Roosevelt army and dedicated it to discipline. Howe, as he had the address's opening paragraph, found the paragraph too rushed, too impersonal. He excised the entire opening sentence: "Our people, now inured to hardship and suffering, do not fear the rigors of discipline." He opted instead for a more tentative approach: "If I read the temper of our people correctly we now realize as have never realized before our interdependence on each other." It was one of the few qualified statements in the speech, but it was a fitting qualifier given what Roosevelt was asking. Moreover, Howe shrewdly invoked one of Roosevelt's favorite campaign themes: economic interdependence. Now, even that theme took on martial implications: "if we are to go forward we must move as a trained and loyal army willing to sacrifice for the good of a common discipline. Because without such discipline no progress is made, no leadership becomes effective." Moley's master term—*discipline*—was still intact, but the "army" of the February 27 draft had become the much more specific "trained and loyal army." This was no mere analogy; it belied none of the hesitation of earlier drafts.

Roosevelt liked the change. He also approved of the more personal appeal to discipline. The Moley-Roosevelt draft had included the somewhat awkward third-person reference: "They are, I know, ready and willing to submit their lives and property to a discipline which aims clearly and honestly at a larger good." Howe liked the appeal but not the pronouns. The sentence now read, "We are, I know, ready and willing to submit our lives and property." If Franklin Roosevelt really was sincere about the depths of the discipline and sacrifice needed to make his leadership effective, he and his troops had to move together, one body, consubstantially—in a unity of duty. The words *they* and *them* had been scrubbed cleanly from the text.

The image of unity was reinforced in a final appeal that Howe left without editorial intervention. Not one of the fifty-six words in the closing had been changed: "We face the arduous days that lie before us in the warm courage of national unity; with the clear consciousness of seeking old and precious moral values; with the clean satisfaction that comes from the stern performance of duty by old and young alike. We aim at the assurance of a rounded and permanent national life." To a prostrate and badly confused people, it was a most reassuring utterance. To a nation still in the throes of a chilling winter, Roosevelt would offer warm courage; to a nation dirty from neglect and wandering, Roosevelt would offer clean satisfaction; and to a purposeless and apprehensive nation, Roosevelt would offer a rounded and permanent national life. It was a most remarkable and apropos vision, a vision that only a supremely confident leader might make.

James MacGregor Burns had been wrong, but only temporarily: The president-elect vigorously crossed out "the temporary humble instrument." He would now be "the present instrument of their wishes."

Roosevelt closed the draft, again, with an eye toward the historical. In pen he wrote, "This was the final draft of the Inaugural at Hyde Park—Wed[nesday] March 1st 1933." Signed Franklin D. Roosevelt.

Unlike the professor, Howe did not keep his drafts. His beloved Franklin should get the credit.

The president-elect had indeed had a busy morning on Wednesday, March 1. He had finished, at least for the time being, his inaugural address. He received Herbert Hoover's latest missive on the gravity of the banking crisis via Secret Service courier; the courier waited as he drafted a brief, noncommittal reply; friends and family continued to gather at Springwood for the early afternoon caravan to the family's residence in New York City; he heard the good news that the House had passed an amendment to the Treasury–Post Office Bill granting him broad powers to reorganize executive agencies. Roosevelt even found time to get his inaugural-day haircut from his "negro" valet, Irvin McDuffie.

Roosevelt kibitzed with the press as he sat in bed receiving his haircut. Press relations between the White House press corps and the president were about to change dramatically—from Hoover's stiff formality and condescension to Roosevelt's gay conviviality. To the assembled group pressed around his bed, Roosevelt mused that he hoped to rent his New York City home while in office. A reporter asked whether he would settle for a four-year or an eight-year lease. The president-elect, not missing a beat, responded in his best gallows humor, "I would be glad to get a one-month lease."

The assembled press also inquired about his inaugural address. While the president-elect would not tip his hand as to contents, he did preview its length. At present, the speech would take twelve minutes to deliver, he reported. However, he hoped to deliver a much shorter version on March 4, somewhere near eight minutes, or only slightly longer than Lincoln's second inaugural address. The reporters would learn, as Ray Moley had, that the president-elect could prevaricate with the best of them.

At about 2:15 in the afternoon, the nation's next president headed south in a caravan of eight cars to the family home at 49 East Sixty-fifth Street. Missing for the short jaunt was Moley. He would meet up with the group from his home base in the city.

Also missing—most conspicuously—was Eleanor.

The months since her husband's election had been marked by profound ambivalence. She had feuded openly with her husband. She knew that her days as a relatively private person were over; particularly upsetting was the realization that her days as a teacher at the Todhunter School, of which she was part proprietor, were over. Following a formal visit with Lou Hoover at the White House, Eleanor was despondent: "I was about to go there to live, and I felt it was anything but marvelous."[3] She recognized that she would need something to occupy her tremendous energies, so upon returning from Washington, D.C., she queried her husband. Would he "like me to do a real job and take over some of his mail." The answer was an emphatic and unequivocal no. After all, "Missy [LeHand] who had been handling his mail for a long time, would feel I was interfering."

Another family conflict, this one far more severe, occurred in late February. Eleanor had no use for preinaugural formalities. She informed her husband that she would drive herself to the capital with a woman friend and her two dogs. The First Lady–elect could manage just fine in her blue Buick convertible. Roosevelt was furious, and Eleanor responded with a fury of her own: Could she not maintain her precious independence for a few more days? The family would be together on the train ride from New York to the capital. Period. Her husband's anger even spilled over into other more official matters. Moley later recalled it was the only time he ever saw Roosevelt get angry about his wife's independent ways. Eleanor finally capitulated.

To make matters worse, her only daughter, Anna Roosevelt Dall, had separated from her husband and was engaged in a less than covert relationship with a similarly separated John Boettiger, a reporter she had met on the campaign trail. Elliott Roosevelt, the couple's twenty-two-year-old son, also kept Eleanor worried with his imminent separation from his wife, Betty Donner, with whom he had had an infant son.

Nevertheless, the contretemps with her husband and the distractions within her own family were tempered by a most unusual and unexpected development: Eleanor was in love. Not unlike her daughter, she had fallen hard for a journalist on the campaign trail, a sturdy-limbed, bright-eyed political reporter from the Associated Press (AP) named Lorena Hickok, or "Hick" as her friends and colleagues called her. Hick, in turn, had fallen just as hard for the soon-to-be First Lady.

If Eleanor's husband had been at all observant, he would have noticed a most conspicuous adornment on his wife's left hand as 1933 dawned: a sapphire and diamond ring Hick had given her as a Christmas present. She had also given Eleanor other "gifts" during the 1932 campaign, during which the two had grown quite intimate.

In a world dominated by men, the hard-working and hard-drinking Hick had won the respect of her fellow journalists. Thanks to her not-insignificant talents and drive, she had earned the prized assignment of covering the Democratic nominee. She was one of only three AP writers awarded such a task. In October, Hick had been reassigned to cover Eleanor when her AP colleague Kay Beebe was given a new assignment. Both Eleanor and Hick were thrilled by the change.

Their relationship had grown from brief flirtations on the campaign trail to extended travels together. Even as Hick's colleagues warned her not to get too close to her sources, she began doing the unthinkable: Her devotion and love for Eleanor were such that she began running her copy through Louis Howe. Had her editors known of this practice, Hick would have been fired on the spot. Howe, of course, bit his lip, for he knew that such press coverage was politically invaluable.

During the interregnum, as Eleanor despaired of her future duties as First Lady, she relied increasingly on Hick. Was it at all surprising that she asked Hick to join her for the trip to meet Lou Hoover? The two had walked together the five blocks from the Presidential Suite at the Mayflower Hotel to the White House. Both understood that their parting that morning outside the steel gates would soon take on more permanence. A First Lady simply could not have such a public relationship—sexual or otherwise—with a prominent political reporter.

Up until the last, she wanted Hick by her side—even if it meant angering her husband. The unidentified "woman friend" of her inaugural traveling plans was, by this time, a foregone conclusion. But even as she reluctantly agreed to travel with her husband, she arranged for Hick to be nearby. She also made secret travel plans, of which no one knew, for March 3. She would need strength, the sort of strength that no human could offer.

Eleanor met up with her husband on Wednesday evening, March 1. Ray Moley put in an appearance as well. He was anxious to see the most recent draft of the address. He was very skeptical that Roosevelt had kept his word. True to form, the speech looked quite different than he recalled seeing it during the early morning hours of February 28. Moley was also anxious about something else, but he did not tell Roosevelt about it.

He had been tendered an offer to write articles about the new administration for a new publication—four short ones or one long article per week. This was precisely the option he had been hoping for as it would allow him to keep his ideological freedom and it would allow him to keep meeting his classes at Columbia. Maybe he would do the assistant secretary of state thing for a month, just enough to aid in the transition and in setting the legislative agenda. Then he could get out. Or, could he? Celeste Jedel, Moley's twenty-one-year-old secretary, saw what perhaps her boss could not: "I feel that once he takes office he won't be able to get out—even if he wants to. F. D. needs him too badly."[4]

News out of Florida on March 2 augured ominously for the Roosevelt administration: Sen. Thomas J. Walsh of Montana, FDR's pick for attorney general, had been found dead by his newlywed wife. The seventy-three-year-old widower had married Señora Mina Nieves Perez Chaumont de Truffin of Havana less than a week earlier. The honeymooners had been headed north, via train, when Mrs. Walsh awoke to find her husband's body in the stateroom, dead from a massive heart attack.

News out of Miami was equally grim. The deathwatch for the mortally wounded mayor, Anton Cermak, had begun; the deathwatch for Giuseppe Zangara, as a result, was also under way.

Finally, the nation's banking infrastructure also seemed to be in its death throes. By Thursday, twenty-one states had declared either total or partial bank holidays. It seemed cruel to declare a holiday that would give millions of depositors across the country little, if any, access to whatever savings the Great Depression had not already ravaged. The holiday would only spread by inaugural morning.

At about 3:30 P.M. on March 2, the president-elect, along with family, friends, advisers, cabinet designees, and the press began the six-hour odyssey to the nation's capital. The security detail was without precedent: In addition to a thirty-three-man police escort on the way to Liberty Street to catch the ferry that would cross the Hudson and meet up with the Baltimore and Ohio rail line, twenty-two hundred uniformed policemen patrolled the route, two hundred plainclothes officers mingled with crowds, and bomb and criminal alien squads had staked out the route. Three hundred additional police officers would monitor the presidential party on the way from the ferry to the terminal of New Jersey's central railroad. Perhaps the nation had suddenly realized the extent to which their fortunes rested on the broad shoulders of the crippled governor. Chance, or was it Divine Intervention, had conspired to allow him to live in Miami. Now, human agency would see to it that he was safely delivered to his destination.

As he settled into his private car, and as the slow but steady clack counted its rhythmic cadence, gravity seemed to descend upon Roosevelt. Instead of sending for Howe, Moley, or even a family member, he sent for Jim Farley—the big, convivial Irish Catholic who had played such an instrumental role in getting him elected, especially in Chicago. For his faithful service, Farley was to be the nation's postmaster general, a position notable for the myriad possibilities of much-coveted patronage. With unemployment nearing 25 percent, Farley could count on being most popular. For now, Roosevelt just wanted his ear.

Farley dropped into a chair next to the president-elect, who sat in an easy chair alongside the living-room wall. The enormity of what he was about to embark upon, the expectations that awaited him from all across the land, summoned up in him the Divine. "You know," Roosevelt mused, "I think a thought to God is the right way to start off my administration. A proper attitude toward religion, and belief in God will in the end be the salvation of all peoples. For ourselves it will be the means of bringing us out of the depths of despair into which so many have apparently fallen."[5] He shared with Farley his plans to have cabinet members and their families join him for morning services at Saint John's Episcopal Church, the church that he had attended for years as assistant secretary of the navy.

As darkness descended along the eastern seaboard, and as the sleet and rain intensified, Eleanor's thoughts turned frequently to Hick, who was riding in a separate car on the B&O. Formalities had stipulated it. Huddled in Hick's lap, though, was Meggie, Eleanor's black Scottish terrier. Eleanor looked forward to being safely ensconced at the Mayflower, where she could again be alone with Hick. She had big plans for the following day.

The train carrying the president-elect's entourage arrived at Union Station at 9:30 P.M. Despite the cold and rain, more than fifteen hundred people had assembled to greet their next president. As they drew to a stop next to the platform, Roosevelt observed the large crowd. His limousine had pulled up close to a special gangplank that would enable him to move quickly from his private railroad car into the backseat without special assistance. As he stepped off the train, the rain suddenly stopped. Flashbulbs exploded. Cheers enveloped him. Secret Servicemen appeared to be everywhere, the pistols in their overcoats hardly inconspicuous.

The presidential cavalcade, with a phalanx of police escorts, moved quickly toward the Mayflower—from Massachusetts Avenue, to H Street, to New York Avenue, onto Pennsylvania Avenue, up Jackson Street, to Seventeenth Street, and finally DeSales Street. Roosevelt entered at the side of the hotel in order to avoid the crowds and undo publicity about his lameness. He and his family, along with the Louis Howes, would occupy the seventh floor.

On her way to the seventh floor, Eleanor had an embarrassing moment—what reporters would call an "inimitable predicament."[6] She had purposefully separated from the presidential throng, ostensibly to check on Meggie. Eleanor, of course, found her. She knew that the dog had been in safe hands; it was Hick she really yearned to see. Once she had located the two of them, she could give the press the requisite excuse. It was duly reported that the next First Lady "had to be escorted in with the puppy on a leash in an arriving party all her own." The presence of Lorena Hickok, a fellow member of the press, was hardly newsworthy.

Before they departed for the evening, however, Eleanor informed Hick of her early morning plans for Friday, March 3. She told Hick to meet her with a cab at a side entrance of the Mayflower at 7:45 A.M. "There will be Secret Service men there," she said, "but I'll tell them you're coming, and I'll try to be just inside the door when you drive up." Eleanor hoped the plan would work: "I don't want to be followed, and that early in the morning I don't think we shall be."

As Eleanor and Hick were planning their morning escape, somewhere in the same city, one of her husband's out-of-town inaugural guests slipped in unobtrusively. Lucy Mercer Rutherfurd, the woman who had caused an irrevocable breach in the Roosevelt's marriage fifteen years earlier, would bear personal witness to her former lover's ascension to power. Back in that troublesome summer of 1918, Roosevelt had given his wife his word that he would never again see his paramour. But words could be facile things to Franklin Roosevelt. Now, at this historic moment, Roosevelt made sure that Lucy would travel to Washington from her winter home in Aiken, South Carolina. Perhaps it was a moment they had once dreamed about, perhaps even together.

Back at the Mayflower, as the evening grew late, Roosevelt consulted with a bevy of advisers. Will Woodin and Moley conferred extensively with him about the devolving banking crisis. Word came from Treasury Secretary Mills that the new administration should declare its intent to control withdrawals of currency and gold. Rather than closing all of the nation's banks, a move favored by the Federal Reserve Board and Treasury Department officials, Hoover hoped that Roosevelt might invoke an arcane statute of the World War I–inspired Trading with the Enemy Act. The statute seemed to give the chief executive authority to curtail the continued runs on gold and currency.

Moley, Woodin, and Roosevelt agreed that there was no need for joint action or for Roosevelt's approval on the matter. Hoover was free to act as he liked; Roosevelt would wait until he was officially sworn in. Before that time, Hoover would have to shoulder the banking burden.

Promptly at 7:45 on Friday morning, a cab wheeled up to the Mayflower's side entrance. Eleanor emerged immediately. She instructed the driver to head toward Rock Creek Cemetery by way of R Street. She wanted to show Hick just where they had lived during the Wilson administration. After passing the house—it had a large sign on the lawn indicating its famous previous occupant—Eleanor lapsed into silence.

At Rock Creek Cemetery, she guided Hick quickly to the enclosed holly grove. Inside was the familiar visage. The two women sat silently on the curved white benches. Hick later recounted: "As I looked at it I felt that all the sorrow humanity had ever had to endure was expressed in that face. I could almost feel the hot stinging unshed tears behind the lowered eyelids."[7] As she gazed up at Saint-Gaudens's masterpiece, the only public mention that Henry Adams ever made of his dead wife, Hick also understood what it was that brought her friend back again and again. "Yet in that expression there was something almost triumphant. There was a woman who had experienced every kind of pain, every kind of suffering ... and had come out of it serene—and compassionate."

The question is, was Hick talking about Grief or her lover? Saint-Gaudens had made the human figure appear androgynous. Why gender it now?

Eleanor finally broke the silence. She spoke solemnly and slowly: "In the old days, when we lived here, I was much younger and not so very wise. Sometimes I'd be very unhappy and sorry for myself." When she felt that way she would "come out here, alone, and sit and look at that woman. And I'd always come away somehow feeling better. And stronger. I've been here many, many times." Eleanor, too, gendered Grief. Perhaps now, more than ever, Eleanor saw her own visage in that veiled, melancholy figure. Like the statue, the elements had aged her, colored her. Although the intervening fifteen years had changed her, there was a solidity and permanence that even the harshest elements could not subdue. It was indeed reassuring. She would survive. She might even triumph. Perhaps Louis Howe had been right all along:

> *Fool! Had you dared to speed your pace*
> *Our masking cowles aside to tear*
> *And meet us bravely face to face*
> *We would have vanished into air.*

Herbert Hoover was in comparatively good spirits. His redemption was now within a day's reach. The hellish bunker that had become the White House would be his burden only a little while longer. His aides and friends had earlier worried among themselves that the presidency might claim yet another victim. The eighteen-hour days, the weight of the nation's proud history, and his own incredibly sensitive emotional mechanism had nearly broken him. Today, however, the end was in sight. The movers had begun packing; Roosevelt could have the job, but not quite yet. He was not yet done with Franklin the trimmer or his New Deal.

Throughout the morning of the third, the president had been buoyed by news conveyed to him by Mills that perhaps a general banking holiday might be avoided. By early afternoon, though, his outlook had changed significantly as reports of massive currency and gold withdrawals flooded in. It was time to play his last card.

It had become customary for the outgoing president to invite his successor to dinner at the White House on the evening of March 3.

Hoover, who abhorred the thought of sharing a meal with the trea-sonous, uncooperative Roosevelt, considered not inviting the president-elect at all. When the chief usher, Ike Hoover (no relation), lobbied for some show of executive diplomacy, Hoover reluctantly agreed to host a late afternoon tea for the Roosevelts.

Franklin and Eleanor arrived at 4 P.M., along with their eldest son, Jimmy, and his wife, Betsy Cushing Roosevelt. Jimmy accompanied his father largely to aid in his locomotion.

As Roosevelt entered the presidential mansion, Ike Hoover whispered to him that the president had invited two additional "guests"—Treasury Secretary Mills and the Federal Reserve Board's Eugene Meyer. After the formalities of tea, Hoover again wanted to press his case for invoking the Trading with the Enemy Act. It amounted to a high-stakes political ambush. Without any of FDR's advisers around to muddy the waters, Hoover figured that they might finally bring the president-elect on board.

Roosevelt barked to the usher, "For God's sake, get Ray."[8]

As Roosevelt was getting the word from the usher, Moley was lying down for a nap. He was exhausted, so much so that paranoia seemed to settle over him. He was even afraid to take off his suit coat for fear that the inaugural address, which he was now "wearing," would fall into the wrong hands. Just as he was about to doze off for a precious few minutes of sleep, the phone in Roosevelt's suite rang. It was the presi-dent-elect's cousin, Warren Delano Robbins, the State Department protocol officer. He relayed to Moley that he was needed at the White House forthwith.

Much to Hoover's consternation, Moley suddenly appeared seconds after Roosevelt called for him following the social amenities. Similar to the night before, Hoover pressed Roosevelt to give him congressional and presidential assurances that he would invoke the Trading with the Enemy Act to regulate the flow of currency and gold. Roosevelt again politely abjured. He was not free to act, Hoover was.

While Roosevelt remained calm throughout the ambush, it became clear that Hoover had reached his tolerance threshold. As the meeting closed, Roosevelt suggested that, given the crisis, if Hoover chose not to return the customary call of the incoming administration, he would understand completely. Hoover could take the diplomatic artifice no longer. For the first time that afternoon, he looked his successor straight in the eye and braced his body. "Mr. Roosevelt, when you are President of the United States for a little while you will come to realize that the President does not call on anybody."

The smile disappeared from Roosevelt's face. "I shall be waiting at my hotel, Mr. President," he responded tersely, "to learn what you decide." With that, he hustled his family out of the Red Room and back to the Mayflower. Jimmy Roosevelt was so angered by Hoover's brazen contempt that his father was sure he "wanted to punch [Hoover] in the eye."[9]

Back at the Mayflower, Roosevelt continued to receive bad news from across the land. By the end of the day, twenty-seven states would either close their banks completely or offer only limited withdrawals. For one of the first times in his memory, Moley noticed that tension was registered on Roosevelt's countenance.

The phone kept ringing in the presidential suite, and party leaders filed in and out, seeking advice and sounding Roosevelt out. Hoover called at 11:30 P.M. to notify Roosevelt that leading bankers from Chicago and New York thought they might be able to survive until the inaugural address, thereby saving themselves further public embarrassment. The president called again at 1 A.M. This time he simply wanted to inform Roosevelt that his men were still working at Treasury, along with officials from the Federal Reserve Board. Roosevelt thanked him for the call. He suggested that he and Hoover both turn in for the evening.

When Moley cleared out of the presidential suite shortly after one he was dead on his feet. Unbeknownst to him, though, his evening was not yet over.

Down the hall, in Eleanor's suite, Lorena Hickok had dined with the lonely First-Lady-to-be. Throughout the long evening, Louis Howe and Jimmy Roosevelt brought them periodic reports of the banking news—all of it bad. Sometime during the evening, her husband sent over a most important document: a final draft of the inaugural address. She read it aloud to Hick. Moley, had he known, would have been beside himself. Roosevelt was basically giving the address to the press with plenty of lead time for the next day's papers. By 1 P.M. the next day, every newspaper in the country could have had a not-so-sneak preview. The effect of the speech, the drama of Roosevelt's carefully cultivated silence, would disappear with a single, simple phone call.

Hick never made it. "There I was, right in the middle of what, that night, was the biggest story in the world. And I did nothing about it."[10] Her allegiance to Eleanor pulled stronger than any speech text, any story, ever could. She later realized that "Lorena Hickok ceased to be a reporter" that night.

Ray Moley stepped out of the elevator into the Mayflower lobby and encountered the administration's treasury secretary designate, Woodin. He could not, in good conscience, head to bed yet, especially given the nature of Hoover's last call. He told Moley that they just had to go over to Treasury and offer their assistance. Moley reluctantly agreed.

They found Mills, Meyer, and several other key Hoover appointees at the Treasury Building. They were desperately trying to get the remaining two holdouts, Illinois and New York, to declare bank holidays, despite the bankers' objections. They had yet to reach Illinois's governor, Henry Horner. Governor Herbert Lehman of New York was reluctant.

During the course of the lengthy telephone negotiations, Ray Moley fell asleep. Woodin awakened him at about 2:30. "It's all right now," he announced. "Everything is closed. Let's go now."

Finally, after nearly four months, the Hoover and Roosevelt forces had achieved some sort of rapprochement at the last hour.

The two exhausted men took a taxi back to the Mayflower. They would have a full day tomorrow. Or was it today?

As he lay down for a few hours sleep, Moley removed the text of the inaugural address from the breast pocket of his suit coat, placed it under his pillow, and promptly nodded off.

CHAPTER NINE

March 4, 1933: *Final Scene*

As the nation awoke on Saturday, March 4, the people's ambivalence was real. Their savings, or what was left of it, had been frozen by edict of the states. One out of every four workers could not find work. All across the country, people wandered, looking for their next meal, searching for that night's lodging. Yet, there was no talk of revolution; that required an expanse of imagination not preoccupied by the mundane details of living. Things had indeed gotten quite basic by inaugural morning.

By a large majority, they had cast their lot four years earlier with a superman, a man who had been sold to the electorate as a technocratic wizard, a master of organization—literally a savior to millions. Even as he entered the White House under such favorable auspices in 1929, Herbert Hoover seemed preternaturally attuned to the expectations his campaign had created. "I have no dread of the ordinary work of the presidency," he confessed to the *Christian Science Monitor*. "What I do fear is the result of the exaggerated idea the people have conceived of me. They have a conviction that I am a sort of superman, that no problem is beyond my capacity." He then eerily forecast the fate of his own presidency: "If some unprecedented calamity should come upon the nation . . . I should be sacrificed to the unreasoning disappointment of a people who expected too much."[1]

Just as the prospects of a Hoover presidency engendered wild optimism in 1929, the nation now turned its hopes to Franklin Roosevelt. They longed for a leader, someone who was not afraid to mix things up. They also yearned to smile again. They had not smiled much during the previous three long years of depression. If their president-elect could grin that big toothy grin with up-thrust jaw, head thrown back, and cigarette holder held at a rakish angle in the darkest days the nation had faced since Lincoln—well, maybe they had cause to smile, too. The nation's journalists sensed a fundamental change of leadership and personality when the president-elect arrived in the capital for the inauguration: "Mr. Roosevelt has the happy faculty of radiating good humor and the Nation is beginning to need that more than ever. . . . It is worth something to the people to have a leader who smiles readily and whose good humor is infectious."[2] The estimable Arthur Krock of the *New York Times* had sensed the basic change of mood as Roosevelt disembarked at Union Station. "From the moment he arrived here, Washington took on almost a visible air of hope."[3] Moreover, that most Hooverian of emotions, confidence, had a cash value firmly attached to it: "he has become a symbol of hope, burning in the darkness that has surrounded us and which has made so many of us afraid. . . . This single fact—this changed state of mind—is in itself of the utmost importance."[4]

As the nation hoped on Saturday morning, as the people prayed for a savior, the man with the crippled body who would shortly inherit their burdens was helped into his clothes.

Franklin Roosevelt's crippled condition also influenced his house of worship that inaugural morning. As he had mentioned to Jim Farley two days earlier, Roosevelt felt it appropriate to begin his administration on a religious note. Months earlier, he had received an invitation from Bishop James E. Freeman to worship at the Washington Cathedral. He politely declined the bishop's invitation. He could not navigate the steep steps leading into the sanctuary. Instead, he selected Saint John's Episcopal Church. In addition to being proximate to the Mayflower and having an easily accessible side entrance, he and his family had worshiped there during his years in the Wilson administration.

Shortly after 10 A.M., with Eleanor, his mother Sara, son Jimmy, and daughter-in-law Betsy, the president-elect headed for Saint John's. Although the temperature was in the thirties, the Roosevelts traveled in an open-canopied car. Nearly a hundred friends, cabinet appointees, relatives, and working associates stood as Roosevelt entered the sanctuary. They returned to their seats when he unfastened his leg braces and had taken his seat near the front. Refereeing the service was his boyhood schoolmaster at Groton, Rev. Endicott Peabody. The rector of Saint John's, Rev. Robert Johnston, assisted the seventy-six-year-old Peabody.

After church hymns were played on the organ and selections had been read from the *Book of Common Prayer,* Reverend Johnston offered a prayer for the nation: "Almighty and most merciful God, grant, we beseech Thee, that by the indwelling of Thy Holy Spirit, Thy servant, Franklin, that he and all his advisors may be enlightened and strengthened for Thy service." Reverend Peabody closed the brief twenty-minute service shortly thereafter with another prayer: "O, Lord, our Heavenly Father, . . . most heartily we beseech Thee, with Thy favor to behold and bless Thy servant, Franklin, chosen to be the President of the United States."[5]

Roosevelt remained on his knees, his face cupped by his hands, several moments after the rector's loud amen. He pulled himself to his feet at 10:40, had his braces locked back into place, and walked with his son as ballast to his waiting car. He had learned the walk seven years earlier while convalescing in Warm Springs. It was a political walk; it could get him a short distance, nothing more. He would use it several times on this most public of days.

Five minutes later, back at the Mayflower Suite, Roosevelt and Moley conferred one final time. The professor briefed FDR on what had happened just hours earlier at the Treasury Department. Roosevelt heartily concurred with what he and Woodin had done. Moley then proposed a three-part postspeech plan of action: declare a national bank holiday, call a special session of Congress to enact emergency banking legislation, and bring the nation's leading bankers to Washington the following day to give advice on shaping such legislation. Roosevelt agreed to each recommendation. To Moley, the irony was palpable: In just a few hours, Roosevelt would castigate the "money changers" who had abdicated their seats in the great temple of finance. Moley was now in charge of seeing to it that those same money changers would soon be on their way back to the temple to advise the new president.

With his assent given, Roosevelt was off. He had one final date to keep with Herbert Hoover. It was a date to which he did not look forward. It was a date he would never forget.

At exactly 10:55 A.M., Roosevelt's open-canopied car arrived at the north entrance of the White House. Cameramen were everywhere, anticipating the ceremonial meeting between the incoming and outgoing presidents, then the brief drive to the Capitol. Its awesome simplicity seemed to symbolize the essence of democratic governance. There was, however, one major problem that morning: Getting in and out of automobiles was terribly awkward for Roosevelt, and this time he could not simply declare to the assembled press corps, as he had countless times before in that avuncular yet vaguely threatening way, "no pictures today, boys." So, he did the only thing he could do, he remained in his car while Eleanor and others in the presidential party waited for the Hoovers in the East Room.

Finally, the Hoovers emerged from the White House's north entrance. Seeing that the president-elect was seated uncomfortably alone in his limousine, Hoover strode briskly over and extended his right hand. For an instant, he seemed to tower over Roosevelt. As his presidency reached its final hours, this handshake marked the extent of his diplomacy. Mills had informed him of the magnanimous gesture made by Woodin and Moley the night before, but that clearly had not changed things. Policy had always been personal to Herbert Hoover, a sentiment largely foreign to his successor, who had flaunted his preferred policies time and again. There would be no rapprochement now—or ever.

The closest thing to diplomacy between Hoover and Roosevelt had happened just hours earlier. On March 3, after the House and Senate finished reconciling a conference report on the Treasury–Post Office Bill, the president had signed into law Title IV of the amendment that would grant his successor vast powers of executive reorganization. It was a bill Hoover had desperately sought during his presidency. A spiteful Congress made sure he did not get it. Instead, it was a generous gift to a man he neither liked nor trusted. Moreover, amid the gravity of the banking crisis and the excitement of a new administration, it was a gift largely forgotten. If Franklin Roosevelt was to be a dictator, as many believed, he had Herbert Hoover largely to thank.

As the seven-car cavalcade pulled out onto Fifteenth Street and then Pennsylvania Avenue, Roosevelt tried repeatedly to break the icy silence that had developed between the two of them. Hoover was not talking, though. Nor was he waving to the estimated half-million people who lined the streets up to eight-deep. He stared straight ahead, his face an inscrutable mask, in a final desperate attempt to ignore the remarkable surroundings.

Roosevelt was also desperate. As their car passed the naked steel girders of what would be the new Commerce Building, Roosevelt heard himself say something bizarre about the "lovely steel."[6] Again, no response. But the response from the crowd-lined streets was overwhelming. So, instead of feigning disinterest, the president-elect did what seemed natural: he doffed his top hat—to the delight of the audience. Hoover did not.

Trailing behind in the next car were Lou Hoover and Eleanor Roosevelt. The incoming First Lady was also anxious to communicate. She asked the outgoing First Lady what she would miss most about not living in the White House. Lou said she would particularly miss the feeling of being taken care of, of not having to make personal plans. Eleanor made a mental note to not become dependent on others. She must continue to do things for herself.

Up ahead, members of the Secret Service detachment were getting increasingly agitated. Through some improbable twists and turns, a taxi carrying three female passengers had inadvertently joined the presidential motorcade. The cab traveled a presidential ten city blocks before it was finally diverted.

At the Capitol, Hoover disembarked quickly. He was in no mood to help the president-elect as he struggled with his leg braces. He walked briskly to the President's Room to do some last-minute bill signing and to greet senators. Roosevelt, on the arm of his eldest son, walked slowly up a specially constructed ramp into the Senate wing of the Capitol. He waited in the Senate Military Affairs Committee room. As he sat quietly and contemplatively in his wheelchair, he took out his copy of the inaugural address. He also took out a pen.

He wanted to convey something of the religiosity of the moment, something to mark this moment as sacred, ordained by the God he had worshiped just an hour and a half earlier. He had felt similarly on the train, in conversation with Farley: God should be invoked from the very outset of his administration. Not in a heavy-handed sort of way, not in an apocalyptic way, not even necessarily in a Judeo-Christian way. At the top of his reading copy he scratched, "This is a day of consecration." With this simple declarative sentence, he closed the drafting process.

At noon, the inaugural committee escorted the president-elect to the Senate chamber to witness the swearing in of his vice president, former Speaker of the House and representative from Texas, John Nance Garner. His mood seemed to lighten as the new senators of the Seventy-third Congress were also sworn in. He chatted jovially with the new Senate majority leader, Joseph Robinson, who was doubling as chairman of the inaugural committee. But it was far from the bonhomie of typical Roosevelt conversation.

At 1 P.M., the dignitaries began to take their place on the canopied inaugural stand. Herbert and Lou Hoover emerged through the crowded East Door and moved down the maroon-carpeted ramp. Eleanor and Sara Roosevelt followed. Seated with the first family was Mrs. Lillian Cross, who had intervened so heroically in Miami. Franklin was wheeled to the entrance where, once again, his leg braces were locked into place. Leaning on the sturdy arm of Jimmy Roosevelt, he made his way slowly to the rostrum where the robed and vandyked Chief Justice of the United States and former governor of New York, Charles Evans Hughes, awaited him. The Marine Band played "Hail to the Chief" to the delight of the hundred thousand spectators assembled on the Capitol lawn.

What those hundred thousand could not see was just how precarious was the oath taking. Roosevelt was unable to stand unassisted, even with leg braces. He had either to be leaning against something or some-one to remain upright. Now, before the nation, he would have to take the oath with his right hand raised and his other hand on the big Dutch family Bible. Even the slightest shift in balance could send the unas-sisted Roosevelt sprawling. One provision that he and Hughes had agreed upon was that Roosevelt would not, like some of his predeces-sors, bend over and kiss the Bible following the oath. Such a kiss would simply be much too risky. The best he could do was practice—and have his son nearby in case something went wrong.

Slowly, carefully, Jimmy Roosevelt made sure that his father was firmly anchored before he backed away. The tan, thick left hand was placed squarely on the open page of I Corinthians chapter 13, the Apostle Paul's famous paean to charity. To the devout, it was a most appropriate selection. To the hardhearted and economic-minded, charities had long since run dry.

At precisely 1:08, in a determined, perhaps grave, voice, Roosevelt repeated after Hughes, "I, Franklin Delano Roosevelt, do solemnly swear that I will faithfully execute the office of President of the United States and will, to the best of my ability, preserve, protect and defend the Con-stitution of the United States, so help me God." A loud, sustained cheer erupted from the gathered multitude.

With the accomplishment of that ceremonial forty-two-word speech act, Franklin Roosevelt became the thirty-second president of the United States. It was a position he would relinquish only in death.

He turned to the podium. Fronting it and almost dwarfing him was a massive eagle, the Great Seal of the United States. The nation's pulse quickened.

President Hoover, Mr. Chief Justice, my friends. This is a day of national consecration, and I am certain that on this day my fellow Americans expect that on my induction into the Presidency I will address them with a candor and a decision which the present situ-ation of our people impels. This is preeminently the time to speak the truth, the whole truth, frankly and boldly. Nor need we shrink from honestly facing conditions in our country today. This great nation will endure as it has endured, will revive, and will prosper. So, first of all, let me assert my firm belief that the only thing we have to fear is fear itself—nameless, unreasoning, unjustified terror which paralyzes needed efforts to convert retreat into advance.

In every dark hour of our national life, a leadership of frankness and of vigor has met with that understanding and support of the people themselves which is essential to victory. And I am convinced that you will again give that support to leadership in these critical days.

In such a spirit on my part and on yours we face our common difficulties. They concern, thank God, only material things. Values have shrunk to fantastic levels, taxes have risen, our ability to pay has fallen, government of all kinds is faced by serious curtailment of income, the means of exchange are frozen in the currents of trade, the withered leaves of industrial enterprise lie on every side, farmers find no markets for their produce, and the savings of many years in thousands of families are gone. More important, a host of unemployed citizens face the grim problem of existence, and an equally great number toil with little return. Only a foolish optimist can deny the dark realities of the moment.

And yet our distress comes from no failure of substance. We are stricken by no plague of locusts. Compared with the perils which our forefathers conquered, because they believed and were not afraid, we have still much to be thankful for. Nature still offers her bounty, and human efforts have multiplied it. Plenty is at our doorstep, but a generous use of it languishes in the very sight of the supply. Primarily, this is because the rulers of the exchange of mankind's goods have failed through their own stubbornness and their own incompetence, have admitted their failure, and have abdicated. Practices of the unscrupulous money-changers stand indicted in the court of public opinion, rejected by the hearts and minds of men.

True, they have tried, but their efforts have been cast in the pattern of an outworn tradition. Faced by failure of credit, they have proposed only the lending of more money. Stripped of the lure of profit by which to induce our people to follow their false leadership, they have resorted to exhortations, pleading tearfully for restored confidence. They only know the rules of a generation of self-seekers. They have no vision, and when there is no vision the people perish.

Yes, the money-changers have fled from their high seats in the temple of our civilization. We may now restore that temple to the ancient truths. The measure of that restoration lies in the extent to which we apply social values more noble than mere monetary profit. Happiness lies not in the mere possession of money; it lies in the joy of achievement, in the thrill of creative effort. The joy, the moral stimulation, of work no longer must be forgotten in the mad chase of evanescent profits. These dark days, my friends, will be worth all they cost us if they teach us that our true destiny is not to be ministered unto but to minister to ourselves, to our fellowmen.

Recognition of that falsity of material wealth as the standard of success goes hand in hand with the abandonment of the false belief that public office and high political position are to be valued only by the standards of pride of place and personal profit. And there must be an end to a conduct in banking and in business which too often has given to a sacred trust the likeness of callous and selfish wrongdoing. Small wonder that confidence languishes, for it thrives only on honesty, on honor, on the sacredness of obligations, on faithful protection, and on unselfish performance. Without them, it cannot live.

Restoration calls, however, not for changes in ethics alone. This nation is asking for action, and action now.

Our greatest primary task is to put people to work. This is no unsolvable problem if we face it wisely and courageously. It can be accomplished in part by direct recruiting by the government itself, treating the task as we would treat the emergency of a war but at the same time, through this employment, accomplishing great—greatly needed projects to stimulate and reorganize the use of our great natural resources.

Hand in hand with that we must frankly recognize the overbalance of population in our industrial centers and by engaging on a national scale in a redistribution endeavor to provide a better use of the land for those best fitted for the land. Yes, the task can be helped by definite efforts to raise the values of agricultural products and with this the power to purchase the output of our cities. It can be helped by preventing realistically the tragedy of the growing loss through forecl—foreclosure of our small homes and our farms. It can be helped by insistence that the Federal, the State, and the local governments act forthwith on the demand that their cost be drastically reduced. It can be helped by the unifying of relief activities which today are often scattered, uneconomical, unequal. It can be helped by national planning for and supervision of all forms of transportation and of communications and other utilities that have a definitely public character. There are many ways in which it can be helped, but it can never be helped by merely talking about it.

We must act, we must act quickly.

And finally, in our progress towards a resumption of work we require two safeguards against a return of the evils of the old order. There must be a strict supervision of all banking and credits and investments. There must be an end to speculation with other people's money. And there must be provision for an adequate but sound currency.

These, my friends, are the lines of attack. I shall presently urge upon a new Congress, in special session, detailed measures for their fulfillment, and I shall seek the immediate assistance of the forty-eight states.

Through this program of action we address ourselves to putting our own national house in order and making income balance outgo. Our international trade relations, though vastly important, are in point of time and necessity secondary to the establishment of a sound national economy. I favor as a practical policy the putting of first things first. I shall spare no effort to restore world trade by international economic readjustment, but the emergency at home cannot wait on that accomplishment. The basic thought that guides these specific means of national recovery is not nationally—narrowly nationalistic. It is the insistence, as a first consideration, upon the interdependence of the various elements in and parts of the United States of America, a recognition of the old and permanently important manifestation of the American spirit of the pioneer. It is the way to recovery. It is the immediate way. It is the strongest assurance that recovery will endure.

In the field of world policy I would dedicate this nation to the policy of the "good neighbor"—the neighbor who resolutely respects himself and, because he does so, respects the rights of others—the neighbor who respects his obligations and respects the sanctity of his agreements in and with a world of neighbors.

If I read the temper of our people correctly, we now realize as we have never realized before our interdependence on each other, that we cannot merely take but we must give as well, that if we are to go forward, we must move as a trained and loyal army, willing to sacrifice for the good of a common discipline, because without such discipline no progress can be made, no leadership becomes effective. We are, I know, ready and willing to submit our lives and our property to such discipline because it makes possible a leadership which aims at the larger good. This I propose to offer, pledging that the larger purposes will bind upon us, bind upon us all as a sacred obligation, with a unity of duty hitherto evoked only in times of armed strife.

With this pledge taken, I assume unhesitatingly the leadership of this great army of our people dedicated to a disciplined attack upon our common problems.

Action in this image, action to this end, is feasible under the form of government which we have inherited from our ancestors. Our constitution is so simple, so practical, that it is possible always to meet extraordinary needs by changes in emphasis and arrangement without loss of essential form. That is why our constitutional system has proved itself the most superbly enduring political mechanism the modern world has ever seen. It has met every stress of vast expansion of territory, of foreign wars, of bitter internal strife, of world relations. And it is to be hoped that the normal balance of executive and legislative authority may be wholly equal, wholly adequate, to meet the unprecedented task before us. But it may be that an unprecedented demand and need for undelayed action may call for temporary departure from that normal balance of public procedure. I am prepared under my constitutional duty to recommend the measures that a stricken nation in the midst of a stricken world may require. These measures, or such other measures as the Congress may build out of its experience and wisdom, I shall seek within my constitutional authority to bring to speedy adoption. But in the event that the Congress shall fail to take one of these two courses, in the event that the national emergency is still critical, I shall not evade the clear course of duty that will then confront me. I shall ask the Congress for the one remaining instrument to meet the crisis: broad executive power to wage a war against the emergency, as great as the power that would be given to me if we were in fact invaded by a foreign foe.

For the trust reposed in me I will return the courage and the devotion that befit the time. I can do no less.

We face the arduous days that lie before us in the warm courage of national unity, with the clear consciousness of seeking old and precious moral values, with the clean satisfaction that comes from the stern performance of duty by old and young alike. We aim at the assurance of a rounded, a permanent national life. We do not distrust the essen—the future of essential democracy. The people of the United States have not failed. In their need they have registered a mandate that they want direct, vigorous action. They have asked for discipline and direction under leadership. They have made me the present instrument of their wishes. In the spirit of the gift, I take it.

In this dedication of a nation, we humbly ask the blessing of God. May he protect each and every one of us. May he guide me in the days to come.[7]

At 1:30 P.M., as the last syllable hung in the air, before the applause could even begin, two men were immediately on their feet. Jimmy Roosevelt quickly secured his father's left arm. To his father's right, a Secret Service agent snatched the speech from the podium. Herbert Hoover was the first to shake the new president's hand. With that gesture, the formalities were officially over. The former president and his wife were hustled to a train headed for New York City and the Waldorf-Astoria. The Marine Band again struck up "Hail to the Chief."

As the applause slowly died down, Ray Moley turned to the woman he was seated next to, the new labor secretary and first woman ever to serve in a presidential cabinet, Frances Perkins, and remarked, "Well, he's taken the ship of state and turned it right around." It was a curious metaphor, one completely foreign to the address. In his year of service, if nothing else, Ray Moley had come to know his man: the navy had never left him, even though he had left it thirteen years earlier.

All across the nation, thousands of Americans immediately sat down with pen and paper and poured out their hearts to a man they felt they now knew intimately. Businessmen, using company stationery, typed out long notes of approbation, and occasionally advice. Even schoolchildren, using lined notebook paper, wrote notes of thanks and hope to their new president. The comparisons were legion: Roosevelt's address was akin to Lincoln's at Gettysburg; he was the new Moses, sent by God to lead His people; he was the new Messiah, sent by God to save the people from themselves. His mandate to lead was divinely sanctioned; the events in Miami bore witness to that. It was an outpouring of affection and intimacy unlike any Washington, D.C., had ever seen.

The nation's press also had a thing or two to say—nearly all of it positive. Even the nation's most stridently Republican papers gave their grudging approval to the tone, if not the substance, of the address. More common were remarks like those that appeared in the *Atlanta Constitution:* "The address takes its place among the greatest of historic State papers of the nation, ranking with Lincoln's address at Gettysburg and the most striking of the war utterances of Woodrow Wilson. No more vital utterance was ever made by a President of the United States."[8]

Perhaps the most immediate widespread opinion about the address engaged yet another irony: the confidence that Herbert Hoover had tried so desperately to create over the past three years had, in the span of about nineteen minutes, miraculously returned. After the address wrote one journalist, "confidence literally arose from its hiding place and is today a living actuality. Confidence has arrived."[9] The editors of the *Hartford Courant* noted, "It is a message that radiates faith, courage and optimism, that stresses moral values and is well calculated to inspire confidence." Sentiments were similar at the *Philadelphia Inquirer:* "All in all, the short inaugural address would have the effect of inspiring confidence in the American people." Journalists at the *Chattanooga Times,* the *Chicago Tribune,* and the *St. Louis Globe Democrat* were in lockstep: "It manifests unwavering faith in America and breathes a spirit of hope and confidence." "President Roosevelt's inaugural strikes the dominant note of courageous confidence." And, "The spirit of courage and confidence with which he addresses his prodigious task is in itself impressive, and particularly so at a time when it is just that spirit which is most needed by the country."

Somewhere in the bold and determined delivery, the carefully worded policies, the assertive and clear statements, the ringing indictments and the promise of immediate action, the American people found reason again to believe, to hope, and to see beyond the bleak landscapes of their own immediate future.

All in just 1,929 words.

Postscript

In his capacity as the president's personal secretary and "man of mystery," Louis Howe moved into the White House in March, 1933. He would not live to see the completion of his beloved Franklin's first term. He went to the grave without ever writing about his long, complex, and intimate relationship with the nation's thirty-second president. To this day, scholars do not know the source of Howe's sublime aphorism, "the only thing we have to fear is fear itself."

Eleanor Roosevelt also moved into the White House, though reluctantly. She was never there very long, as her journeys around the country soon became something of a national expectation. In so doing, she redefined the role of First Lady. She would return occasionally to Rock Creek Cemetery and "Grief." She also maintained a thirty-year relationship with Lorena Hickok. Unfortunately, Hick destroyed much of their correspondence.

Herbert Hoover moved out of the White House into a residence he would maintain for more than thirty years at New York's Waldorf-Astoria Hotel. He also maintained a residence at his beloved alma mater, Stanford University, in Palo Alto, California. Franklin Roosevelt never called on his expertise—in peace or war. While the years eventually softened some of his animosity toward Roosevelt, he never outlived his legacy as the do-nothing president who presided over the Great Depression. He still has not.

Raymond Moley eventually left the Roosevelt administration. In July, 1933, the president betrayed his trust for the last time, at of all places, ironically, the London Economic Conference. In September, he officially resigned his position as assistant secretary of state. He became a writer and editor for a new weekly magazine, *Today,* which eventually merged with *Newsweek.* He also continued to teach at Columbia. He would occasionally work with Roosevelt on drafting speeches during his first term. During Roosevelt's second term, he became disillusioned with his policies and was publicly critical of the administration and the president. He later found a friend in Herbert Hoover. They struck up an affectionate and warm relationship. At the close of his long life, he gave his papers to the Hoover Institution on War, Revolution, and Peace at Stanford University. Included in those papers are his notes and drafts of the inaugural address.

Franklin Roosevelt became the nation's only four-term president, and his stature as the twentieth century's most important president remains uncontested. It was through the spoken word, carried by radio, that he endeared himself to millions of Americans. While he gave scores of memorable speeches, his first inaugural address stands without rival for its artistry and its impact. He remained personally affable, yet terribly private, until his death in April, 1945. He spent the last years of his life as a very lonely man. Lucy Mercer Rutherfurd was with him at Warm Springs when he suffered a massive cerebral hemorrhage and died at the age of sixty-three.

Notes

Chapter One. March 4, 1933

1. For the personal responses sent to Franklin D. Roosevelt's first inaugural address, see President's Personal File, box 200B, "Personal Reactions, March 4, 1933," containers 6, 7, and 8, Franklin D. Roosevelt Presidential Library, Hyde Park, N.Y. (hereafter FDR Library).

Chapter Two. September 22, 1932

1. Adolf Berle Jr., "Memorandum to Governor Franklin D. Roosevelt," box 15, "Memoranda from Campaign," Berle Papers, FDR Library.
2. Interview with Raymond Moley by Elliott Rosen, Oral History Series, Herbert Hoover Presidential Library, West Branch, Iowa (hereafter Hoover Library), 1–3.
3. Raymond Moley, *After Seven Years*, 1.
4. Raymond Moley to Nell Moley, Apr. 12, 1932, box 38-43, "Indexed Correspondence," Raymond Moley Papers, Hoover Institution on War, Revolution, and Peace, Stanford University, Stanford Calif. (hereafter Moley Papers).
5. Raymond Moley, *The First New Deal*, 98.
6. Ibid., 99.

Chapter Three. November 8, 1933

1. "Roosevelt, Franklin D.—Campaign Plans, Notes of Raymond Moley, 1932," Box 282-13, "F. D. Roosevelt Schedule A," Moley Papers.
2. Herbert C. Hoover, *Public Papers of the Presidents of the United States, 1932–33*, 804–805.

3. Quoted in Alfred B. Rollins Jr., *Roosevelt and Howe*, 363.
4. Quoted in Eleanor Roosevelt, *This I Remember*, 74.
5. Quoted in Blanche Wiesen Cook, *Eleanor Roosevelt*, vol. 1, *1884–1933*, 446.
6. Quoted in ibid., 472.
7. Quoted in ibid., 247.
8. Quoted in ibid., 236.
9. Quoted in Frank Freidel, *Franklin D. Roosevelt: The Triumph*, 371.
10. Poem from Louis Howe to Eleanor Roosevelt, Dec. 1931, box 8, "General Correspondence, 1928–1932," Eleanor Roosevelt Papers, FDR Library (hereafter Eleanor Roosevelt Papers).
11. Poem from Louis Howe to Eleanor Roosevelt, Jan. 1, 1932, ibid.

Chapter Four. November 22, 1932

1. Moley, *After Seven Years*, 67.
2. Raymond Moley to Louis Howe, Nov. 12, 1933, box 24, "Indexed Correspondence," file 30, Moley Papers.
3. Hoover, *Public Papers*, 815.
4. Ibid., 816.
5. Quoted in Frank Freidel, *Franklin D. Roosevelt: Launching the New Deal*, 27.
6. Hoover, *Public Papers*, 822.
7. Quoted in Moley, *After Seven Years*, 75.
8. Hoover, *Public Papers*, 826.
9. Quoted in Moley, *First New Deal*, 29.
10. John Maynard Keynes, *The Economic Consequences of the Peace*.
11. Cited in Timothy Walch and Dwight M. Miller, eds., *Herbert Hoover and Franklin D. Roosevelt: A Documentary History*, 5–6.
12. Cited in ibid., 24.
13. Cited in ibid., 32.
14. This incident is detailed by Eleanor Roosevelt in *This I Remember*, 61–62.
15. Diary entry, Feb. 7, 1932, Theodore G. Joslin Papers, box 10, Hoover Library.
16. This episode is recounted in a diary entry of July 2, 1932, James H. McLafferty Papers, box 2, Hoover Institution on War, Revolution, and Peace, Stanford University, Stanford Calif. (hereafter McLafferty Diary).
17. Quoted in Kenneth S. Davis, *FDR: The New York Years, 1928–1933*, 256.

Chapter Five. February 12–13, 1933

1. Moley, *After Seven Years,* 80.
2. Quoted in ibid., 81.
3. Hoover, *Public Papers,* 910.
4. Ibid., 911, 912.
5. Ibid., 912, 913.
6. Ibid., 913, 914.
7. Raymond Moley Diary, Jan. 21, 1933, maintained by Celeste Jedel, box 1, Moley Papers (hereafter Moley Diary).
8. Moley *After Seven Years,* 106.
9. Ibid., 116.
10. F. D. Roosevelt, Schedule A, box 289-5, "Roosevelt, Franklin D. Inaugural Address, March 4, 1933," Moley Papers.
11. Box 289-5, Moley Papers.
12. *Congressional Record—Senate,* February 2, 1933, vol., 76, pt. 3, 72d Cong., 2d sess., (Jan. 24, 1933–Feb. 4, 1933): 3160.
13. Box 289-5, Moley Papers.
14. Box 289-5, Moley Papers.
15. Box 289-5, Moley Papers.
16. Quoted in Cecil B. Dicrson, "Garner Proposes to Put all Funds Under President," *Atlanta Constitution,* Feb. 10, 1933, 1, 7.
17. Quoted in the Kyle D. Palmer, "Dictator Move Hit," *Los Angeles Times,* Feb. 11, 1933, 1, 2.
18. Hiram Johnson, Feb. 12, 1933, in *The Diary Letters of Hiram Johnson,* vol. 5, *1929–1933,* n.p.
19. Box 289-5, Moley Papers.

Chapter Six. February 15–17, 1933

1. Moley, *After Seven Years,* 122.
2. Moley Diary, Feb. 13, 1933.
3. Quoted in Freidel, *Launching the New Deal,* 169.
4. Quoted in ibid.
5. Quoted in Moley, *First New Deal,* 66.

6. Franklin D. Roosevelt, "Informal Extemporaneous Remarks at Miami, Fla., Immediately Preceding Attempted Assassination of the President-Elect," Feb. 15, 1933, in *The Public Papers and Addresses of Franklin D. Roosevelt*, vol. 1, 889–90.

7. Quoted in Blaise Picchi, *The Five Weeks of Giuseppe Zangara*, 16.

8. Quoted in Freidel, *Launching the New Deal*, 170.

9. Raymond Moley to Fred Charles, Feb. 24, 1933, box 65, "Indexed Correspondence," file 3, Moley Papers.

10. "The Presidency," *Time*, Feb. 27, 1933, 7.

11. F. D. Roosevelt, Schedule A.

12. "To Hand F.D.R. the Economy Ax," *Literary Digest*, Feb. 25, 1933, 7.

13. Franklin D. Roosevelt, "I Believe that the Best Interests of the Country Require a Change in Administration," campaign address at Madison Square Garden, New York, N.Y., Nov. 5, 1932, in *Public Papers and Addresses*, 1:862.

14. Herbert Hoover to Franklin D. Roosevelt, Feb. 18, 1933, "Herbert Hoover 1933–1944 and Cross-References," FDR Library.

15. Hoover, *Public Papers*, 1042.

16. Ibid., 1043.

17. Ibid., 1056.

18. Ibid., 1057.

19. Herbert Hoover to Franklin D. Roosevelt, Feb. 28, 1933, "Herbert Hoover 1933–1944 and Cross References," FDR Library.

20. Hoover, *Public Papers*, 1061.

21. Ibid., 1060.

Chapter Seven. February 27–28, 1933

1. James MacGregor Burns, *Roosevelt: The Lion and the Fox*, 161.

2. Quoted in Davis, *FDR*, 334.

3. Moley Diary, Feb. 27, 1933.

4. Franklin D. Roosevelt, handwritten draft of inaugural address, speech files 610–614, container 13, FDR Library.

5. Moley, *First New Deal*, 114.

6. Quoted in "Grave Problems the New President Faces," *Literary Digest*, Mar. 4, 1933, 7.

7. "Governor's Roosevelt's Campaign," *Nation*, Nov. 2, 1932, 414.

8. Roosevelt, handwritten draft of inaugural address.

9. McLafferty Diary, Jan. 15 and Apr. 21, 1932.

10. F. D. Roosevelt, Schedule A.

11. Franklin D. Roosevelt, "I Pledge You—I Pledge Myself to a New Deal for the American People," nomination acceptance speech, Chicago, July 2, 1932, in *Public Papers and Addresses*, 1:659.

12. Franklin D. Roosevelt, Nov. 7, 1932, speech at Poughkeepsie, N.Y., reprinted in Moley, *After Seven Years*, 402.

Chapter Eight. February 28–March 3, 1933

1. Moley Diary, Mar. 1, 1933.

2. Franklin D. Roosevelt, draft of first inaugural address, Mar. 1, 1933, speech file 610, container 13, FDR Library.

3. Roosevelt, *This I Remember*, 76.

4. Moley Diary, Mar. 3, 1933.

5. Quoted in James Farley, *Jim Farley's Story: The Roosevelt Years*, 36.

6. "Roosevelt and Family Reach Capital for Inauguration," *New York Times*, Mar. 3, 1933, 8.

7. Quoted in Blanche Wiesen Cook, *Eleanor Roosevelt*, 1:492.

8. Moley Diary, Mar. 3, 1933.

9. Quoted in Grace Tully, *FDR: My Boss*, 64.

10. Quoted in Rodger Streitmatter, ed., *Empty Without You: The Intimate Letters of Eleanor Roosevelt and Lorena Hickok*, 13.

Chapter Nine. March 4, 1933: Final Scene

1. Quoted in David Burner, *Herbert Hoover: A Public Life*, 211.

2. "Difficulties and Hopes," *Patriot* (Harrisburg, Pa.), Mar. 4, 1933, 8.

3. Arthur Krock, "Roosevelt Arrival Heartens Capitol," *New York Times*, Mar. 3, 1933, 2.

4. "The Return of Hope," *Pittsburgh Press*, Mar. 3, 1933, 1.

5. "Roosevelt Busy from Dawn to Night," *New York Times*, Mar. 5, 1933, 2.

6. Roosevelt, *This I Remember*, 77.

7. Franklin D. Roosevelt, "Inaugural Address," Mar. 4, 1933, Video recording, Great Speeches, Vol. V, Educational Video Group, 1989.

8. Newspaper reactions to the address can be found in the *Washington Post,* Mar. 5, 1933.

9. Robert L. Vann, "Confidence Has Arrived," *Pittsburgh Press,* Mar. 11, 1933, 1.

Bibliography

Manuscript Sources

Berle, Adolph A. Jr. Papers. Franklin D. Roosevelt Presidential Library. Hyde Park, New York.

Hoover, Herbert C. Papers. Herbert Hoover Presidential Library. West Branch, Iowa.

Howe, Louis McHenry. Papers. Franklin D. Roosevelt Presidential Library. Hyde Park, New York.

Joslin, Theodore. Papers. Herbert Hoover Presidential Library. West Branch, Iowa.

McLafferty, James H. Papers. Hoover Institution on War, Revolution, and Peace. Stanford University, Stanford California.

Moley, Raymond. Oral History. Herbert Hoover Presidential Library. West Branch, Iowa.

———. Papers. Hoover Institution on War, Revolution, and Peace. Stanford University, Stanford, California.

Roosevelt, Eleanor. Papers. Franklin D. Roosevelt Presidential Library. Hyde Park, New York.

Roosevelt, Franklin D. Papers. Franklin D. Roosevelt Presidential Library. Hyde Park, New York.

Published Sources

Burner, David. *Herbert Hoover: A Public Life.* New York: Knopf, 1979.

Burns, James MacGregor. *Roosevelt: The Lion and the Fox.* New York: Harcourt, Brace, 1956.

————, and Susan Dunn. *The Three Roosevelts*. New York: Atlantic Monthly Press, 2001.

Daughton, Suzanne M. "Metaphorical Transcendence: Images of the Holy War in Franklin Roosevelt's First Inaugural." *Quarterly Journal of Speech* 79 (1993): 427–46.

Davis, Kenneth S. *FDR: The New York Years, 1928–1933*. New York: Random House, 1985.

Farley, James. *Jim Farley's Story: The Roosevelt Years*. New York: McGraw-Hill, 1948.

Farrell, Thomas B. *Norms of Rhetorical Culture*. New Haven, Conn.: Yale University Press, 1993, 83–93.

Freidel, Frank. *Franklin D. Roosevelt: The Triumph*. Boston: Little, Brown, 1956.

————. *Franklin D. Roosevelt: Launching the New Deal*. Boston: Little, Brown, 1973.

Friedrich, Otto. *Clover*. New York: Simon and Schuster, 1979.

Herring, E. Pendleton. "Second Session of the Seventy-second Congress, December 5, 1932, to March 4, 1933." *American Political Science Review* 27 (1933): 404–22.

Hoover, Herbert C. *Public Papers of the Presidents of the United States, 1932–33*. Washington, D. C: Government Printing Office, 1977.

Houck, Davis W. *Rhetoric as Currency: Hoover, Roosevelt, and the Great Depression*. College Station: Texas A&M University Press, 2001.

Johnson, Hiram. *The Diary Letters of Hiram Johnson, 1917–1945*. Ed. Robert E. Burke. New York: Garland, 1983.

Kearns Goodwin, Doris. *No Ordinary Time*. New York: Simon and Schuster, 1994.

Kennedy, David M. *Freedom From Fear: The American People in Depression and War, 1929–1945*. New York: Oxford University Press, 1999.

Keynes, John Maynard. *The Economic Consequences of the Peace*. New York: Harcourt, Brace, and Howe, 1920.

Moley, Raymond. *After Seven Years*. New York: Harper and Brothers, 1939.

————. *The First New Deal*. New York: Harcourt, Brace and World, 1966.

Picchi, Blaise. *The Five Weeks of Giuseppe Zangara*. Chicago: Academy, 1998.

Rollins, Alfred B. Jr. *Roosevelt and Howe*. New York: Knopf, 1962.

Roosevelt, Eleanor. *This I Remember*. New York: Harper and Brothers, 1949.

Roosevelt, Elliott, and James Brough. *An Untold Story: The Roosevelts of Hyde Park*. New York: Putnam, 1973.

Roosevelt, Franklin D. *The Public Papers and Addresses of Franklin D. Roosevelt*. Vols. 1 and 2. Ed. Samuel I. Rosenman. New York: Random House, 1938, 1939.

Ryan, Halford Ross. "Roosevelt's First Inaugural: A Study of Technique." *Quarterly Journal of Speech* 65 (1979): 137–49.

Schlesinger, Arthur M. Jr. *The Crisis of the Old Order, 1919–1933*. Boston: Houghton Mifflin, 1957.

Streitmatter, Rodger, ed. *Empty Without You: The Intimate Letters of Eleanor Roosevelt and Lorena Hickok*. New York: Free Press, 1998.

Tully, Grace. *FDR: My Boss*. Chicago: Peoples, 1949.

Walch, Timothy, and Dwight M. Miller. *Herbert Hoover and Franklin D. Roosevelt: A Documentary History*. Westport, Conn.: Greenwood, 1998.

Wiesen Cook, Blanche. *Eleanor Roosevelt*. Vol. 1, *1884–1933*. New York: Viking, 1993.

———. *Eleanor Roosevelt*. Vol. 2, *1933–1938*. New York: Viking, 1999.

Index

ISBN 1-58544-198-8

90000